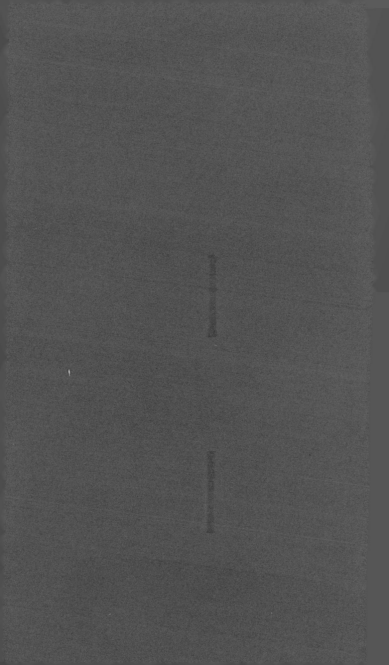

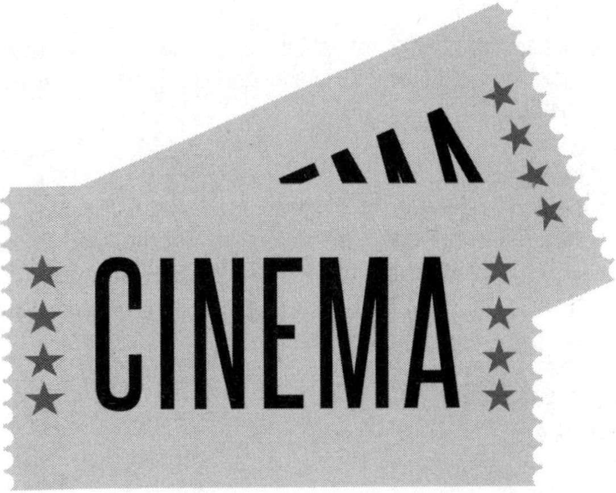
CINEMA

CINEMA: From the Silent Screen to the Hollywood Blockbuster

Summersdale Publishers Ltd
46 West Street
Chichester
West Sussex
PO19 1RP
UK

www.summersdale.com

Printed and bound in the Czech Republic

ISBN: 978-1-84953-720-9

Substantial discounts on bulk quantities of Summersdale books are available to corporations, professional associations and other organisations. For details contact Nicky Douglas by telephone: +44 (0) 1243 756902, fax: +44 (0) 1243 786300 or email: nicky@summersdale.com.

CINEMA

FROM THE SILENT SCREEN TO THE HOLLYWOOD BLOCKBUSTER

GRAHAM TARRANT

summersdale

For my three leading ladies:
Abigail, Francesca and Rose.

CONTENTS

INTRODUCTION

On my first few visits to the cinema – I was six or seven at the time and accompanied by my parents – nervous anticipation caused me to throw up, with the result that I never managed to see a film all the way through until I was into double figures. I like to think it was an early airing of my critical faculties, as I've walked out of a few movies since, but in truth it was simply the excitement of being in that magical environment, an element of which has never left me. By the time I hit my teens I was an avid movie fan and once spent a wet day (and night) in London sitting through the programmes at five different cinemas back to back.

Nowadays these former 'picture palaces' are just one of the viewing options open to the moviegoer. Films can be watched on planes, trains and in cars (providing somebody else is driving); on televisions, laptops, iPads and mobile phones – though surely

only those desperate for a cinematic fix resort to the latter. The point is that for many people viewing a film has become a solitary experience, like listening to music or reading a book. But if watching movies isn't quite the communal event that it used to be, it is certainly no less miraculous.

At the throat-lumping climax of *Casablanca*, Humphrey Bogart reassures a tearful Ingrid Bergman that 'we'll always have Paris'. More importantly, for those of us mistily watching the scene for the umpteenth time, is that we'll always have *Casablanca* – and much more besides. Thanks to the miracle of film (and the supporting technology of DVDs and downloads) we shall always have the curvaceous charms of Marilyn Monroe and the rebellious spirit of James Dean; a pigtailed Judy Garland will always be waiting for us on the Yellow Brick Road and John Wayne will forever be doing what a man's got to do. We can dip at random into half a century of Jack Nicholson or Michael Caine, or let the force of *Star Wars* be with us over and over again. Favourite movies from *Brief Encounter* to *The Hunger Games* can be digitally stored in a personal archive, to be viewed whenever the mood takes us.

Film-making is a protracted, costly and often tedious affair, with longueurs that sometimes drive actors in particular to distraction (having spent a year on the west coast of Ireland shooting David Lean's 1969 epic *Ryan's Daughter*, actor Leo McKern commented 'I don't like to be paid £500 a week for sitting down and playing Scrabble.'). It can be a physically hazardous occupation with actors and, more predictably, stunt personnel being frequent casualties, along with cameramen and even directors. The financial rewards of course can be breathtaking but there are also damaging losses, to reputations as well as to bank balances. None of this need worry the movie fan, however, who can just sit back and enjoy the finished product – or not, as the case may be.

'Let's Go to the Movies' sing 'Daddy' Warbucks and the young eponymous heroine of the 1982 musical *Annie*. It's a fine idea – and the underlying message of this book. Cinema has created a galaxy of stars (and superstars) since its tentative beginnings a hundred or so years ago. Countless directors, writers, composers, artists, cameramen and other technicians have displayed their distinguished talents on the big screen. Only a few can be mentioned in this brief celebration of cinema, though hopefully enough to send moviegoers down some hitherto unfamiliar paths.

In the year between writing this book and its publication thousands of new films will have been produced (close to 600 in Hollywood alone, though that is only half the annual output of India's vast movie industry). Not all of them will get distribution or be worth watching, but plenty will. Some may in time become classics, others will certainly warrant a second or third viewing. Happily, our appetite for cinema shows little sign of diminishing, with a new crop of movies to feast on every year.

CHAPTER 1

THE FLICKERING IMAGE

Of all the arts, the cinema is the most important for us.
VLADIMIR ILYICH LENIN

The American Thomas Alva Edison has harvested most of the credit for inventing moving pictures, though in fact it was a collaborative effort involving many European pioneers over a period of half a century or more. Indeed the process might be said to have started with the development of the magic lantern in the seventeenth century.

In 1876, Edison had come up with the phonograph. Now, with his brilliant assistant W. K. Laurie Dickson alongside (some film historians believe the bulk of the credit should indeed go to Dickson), he threw himself into the task of inventing a visual equivalent, a mechanical device that would project moving pictures.

The result of their combined endeavours, the kinetoscope, went on display in 1894 and took America by storm. The breakthrough had come a few years earlier with the development by Eastman Kodak of flexible celluloid film, the use of which was crucial to Edison's design. By looking through the peephole of the machine the viewer could see images of people or things in motion. It was jerky and grainy, but it was a *moving* picture.

The zoetrope

In 1834 a British mathematician, William George Horner, created the zoetrope (from the Greek zoe, meaning 'life', and tropos, 'turning'). Horner's popular optical toy was in the form of an open-topped cylinder or drum, with a number of equally spaced vertical slits around the side. On the inner surface of the drum was a sequence of pictures. As the drum revolved the viewer peered through the slits at the pictures opposite, the rotating images giving the illusion of moving action. When Francis Ford Coppola and George Lucas set up their Californian film company in 1969, they called it American Zoetrope.

Moving pictures

Hundreds of kinetoscopes flooded onto the market and were set up in penny arcades and peep-show parlours. The visual content, produced in Edison's own studio, included erotic dances, slapstick routines and boxing bouts. With people queuing up to view at a penny a pop, the money poured in, and Edison the businessman was at first content to leave it at that, believing that to project his 'movies' onto a larger screen for an audience to see together would simply reduce the market. However, as others moved in to capitalise on his invention and projection equipment improved, Edison changed tactics and sanctioned the screening of his material, initially in vaudeville theatres where for a while the new attraction eclipsed even the most celebrated stage acts.

European pioneers weren't far behind, with Robert Paul in London and the Lumière brothers in Paris heading the pack. Auguste and Louis Lumière had been in the photographic business for years with a large factory in Lyon. In 1895, in the spacious basement of the Grand Café in Paris, they staged 'Lumière's Cinematograph': a programme of ten short scenes, each a few minutes in length, filmed in and around Lyon. The audience was astonished and thrilled in equal measure, watching the humdrum daily events on the screen as if they were miracles from on high.

Fire hazard

Paris was the scene of cinema's first major tragedy. In 1897 a demonstration of the cinematograph, a combined motion picture camera and projector recently invented in France, was the highlight of a large charity bazaar in the nation's capital. The cream of Parisian society attended the event, which took place in a low-slung wooden building specially constructed for the occasion. The projectionist's assistant struck a match while a lamp nearby was being filled with ether. Within minutes the building was an inferno. The death toll was a shocking 121.

The nickelodeon

By the turn of the century vaudeville theatres had largely given up on showing moving pictures and reverted to their staple music-hall fare. New venues, typically small halls or converted stores, began to crop up throughout urban America. They became known as nickelodeons, so-called because the entrance fee was five cents (a nickel). Many of the early establishments were dingy, cramped and smelly, often a haven for drunks and tramps. But standards gradually improved and for a city's poorest class, which included a swelling number of immigrants, the nickelodeon became a welcome – and often informative – distraction from the miserable daily grind (the rural population had to make do with travelling film shows, if anything at all). A show lasted a mere 15 to 20 minutes, much of it just filmed fragments, and it soon became clear that something more substantial was needed to satisfy the audience's growing appetite.

Groundbreakers

The lead came from France in the person of Georges Méliès, a popular stage magician and proprietor of a theatre in Paris, who saw the possibilities of film as an extension of the world of illusion. Practising with a camera acquired from Louis Lumière, he conjured up various innovative techniques, including the dissolve, fade-out, fast and slow motion, and double exposure – though the latter probably happened more by luck than judgement. He began to make films that told stories, starting in 1900 with a truncated version of *Cinderella*. Two years later came *Le voyage dans la lune* (*The Trip to the Moon*), inspired by the novels of Jules Verne and H. G. Wells. It was the way forward.

The Great Train Robbery, made in 1903 by Edwin S. Porter, is recognised as America's first real movie. Lasting just 11 minutes and shot in New Jersey, it is a story of the Wild West and packs a lot of action into its brief span. Porter, who was both director and cameraman, used a number of new techniques in making the film, which was predictably a huge success and followed on from his even shorter but equally inventive *Life of an American Fireman*. Storytelling now became a feature of American films but, despite Porter's lead, most productions were very stagy with actors shot full length by a camera in a fixed position. In the absence of dialogue the characters gesticulated in an exaggerated fashion and what subtitles there were added little to the audience's appreciation of what they were watching.

It was time for the new medium to find a style of its own.

The Birth of a Nation

Kentucky-born David Wark Griffith became the most influential film-maker of his time. He made over a hundred one-reel films for the Biograph Company, taking the medium to another level and in the process recruiting a roster of young actors who would go on to become stars of the silent screen. It was D. W. Griffith who first changed the camera angle during the course of a scene and introduced the close-up, thus ridding performances of much of their theatricality. His close collaborator in all of this was cameraman G. W. ('Billy') Bitzer. Developing his narrative technique, Griffith moved on to two-reelers (20 minutes of screen time), though the bosses at Biograph feared that anything longer would exhaust the audience's interest.

In 1913, frustrated by Biograph's reluctance to invest in bigger productions, Griffith switched companies and headed out to Hollywood to make America's first major epic, *The Birth of a Nation*. Based on Thomas E. Dixon's successful novel *The Clansman*, the film tells the story of the American Civil War and its aftermath, but from a distinctly Southern perspective. Amazingly, given its battle scenes and many different locations, the entire film (all 165 minutes of it) was shot with one camera and by one cameraman, the formidable Billy Bitzer. For one sequence Bitzer had to lie flat on the ground operating his camera while horses leapt over him. The film opened in New York in 1915 and was a sensational success.

Presidential rating

The Birth of a Nation *was the first film ever to be shown at the White House. President Woodrow Wilson, who was given a private viewing in March 1915, was hugely impressed with the film, commenting afterwards: 'It is like writing history with lightning, and my one regret is that it is all so terribly true.' It was a statement he would come to regret when the film was heavily criticised for its denigrating portrayal of the black community and its glorification of the Ku Klux Klan.*

Hooray for Hollywood

The movie business (not yet an industry) had been mainly centred in New York and in West Orange, New Jersey, where the Edison studio was located. In 1909 a Chicago filmmaker, Colonel William Selig (the title was phoney), built Hollywood's first studio on the site of a Chinese laundry. The climate, space and cheap real estate were powerful inducements and more and more companies transferred to the Californian sunshine. Universal was the first major studio to set up shop there, in 1915. Paramount, Fox, United Artists, Warner Brothers, MGM and Columbia followed over the next few years.

Their stars became household names – from the Latin lover Rudolph Valentino to the slapstick duo Laurel and Hardy; from the swashbuckling Douglas Fairbanks to the gunslinging Tom Mix; from 'America's sweetheart' Mary Pickford to the 'It Girl' Clara Bow. Many actors destined to become superstars in talkies cut their teeth in silent films – Clark Gable, Gary Cooper, Cary Grant, Marlene Dietrich and Greta Garbo among them.

The lure of fame and fortune had actors and aspiring actors flooding into Hollywood, along with writers, directors, artists, stuntmen and all manner of hangers-on. Everybody, it seemed, wanted to work in the film factory.

Exit Rudy

More than 100,000 people, most of them women, lined the streets of New York in August 1926 for the funeral of Rudolph Valentino, the 'Great Lover' of the silent screen. Several female fans, and at least one male, committed suicide. Distraught women stormed the funeral chapel where his body lay at rest and had to be forcibly rebuffed by police. The actor's coffin was surrounded by an honour guard of young men dressed Fascist-style in black shirts, alongside them lay a large wreath purportedly from the Italian dictator Mussolini, inscribed 'From Benito' – a publicity stunt drummed up by the funeral home's press agent.

Silent classics

Directors, many of whom would be making films for decades to come, were learning their craft on the job and producing some landmark movies in the process. Foremost among them was Cecil B. DeMille, a stage actor before switching to a career behind the camera. DeMille directed the first feature-length film to be shot in Hollywood itself, *The Squaw Man* (1914), a Western that he would go on to remake twice: first in 1918, again as a silent film, and then in 1931 as a talkie. He pioneered the biblical epic with his mammoth productions of *The Ten Commandments* (1923) and *The King of Kings* (1927), about Jesus Christ, spectacularly bringing to life stories that his cinema audience had grown up with. He successfully returned to the story of *The Ten Commandments* in 1956, this time in colour and with sound, and with Charlton Heston as Moses. DeMille, an inveterate showman, appeared as himself in Billy Wilder's 1950 classic *Sunset Boulevard*, in which Gloria Swanson, a star of the silent era (both in the film and in real life) has the immortal line: 'All right, Mr DeMille, I'm ready for my close-up.'

Europe's film industry wasn't far behind (indeed it was sometimes ahead), producing in the twenties some of cinema's all-time classics. Robert Wiene's *The Cabinet of Dr. Caligari*, made in Germany in 1920, has been described as the first true horror film. Seven years later another German director, Fritz Lang (who would move to Hollywood and make many distinguished films there), created the visionary sci-fi feature, *Metropolis*. From the Soviet Union came Sergei Eisenstein's revolutionary masterpiece *The Battleship Potemkin* (1925), with its famous Odessa Steps sequence, while the French actor and director Abel Gance turned the spotlight on another period of history with his monumental epic *Napoleon* (1927). In the UK a promising young director made his mark with a tense thriller called *The Lodger* (1926). His name was Alfred Hitchcock.

Sweeping clean

In the 1920s, Hollywood was rocked by a series of scandals. One of its foremost comedy stars, the oversize Roscoe 'Fatty' Arbuckle, was arrested on a rape charge following the death of a young actress named Virginia Rappe during a 48-hour orgy at a San Francisco hotel. A few months later, in February 1922, director William Desmond Taylor was murdered at his luxurious Beverly Hills home. Police discovered a cache of pornography and evidence of sexual involvement with two movie favourites, Mabel Normand and Mary Miles Minter, including a closet full of the latter's monogrammed underwear. The following year, the popular star Wallace Reid died in a padded cell, a victim of drug addiction. No one was ever convicted for the Taylor murder and, after three trials in four months, Roscoe Arbuckle was declared innocent, though the scandal destroyed his career.

The public backlash against the industry alarmed studio bosses, who decided to recruit someone to clean up Hollywood's act. The man they chose was Will H. Hays, a Presbyterian elder and former Postmaster General in the American government. The self-righteous, narrow-minded lawyer was given a free hand by his employers. He had 'morality clauses' written into actors' contracts threatening termination for any transgression. More damagingly, he introduced a sweeping code of censorship that unhealthily sanitised film production and promotion. The so-called Production Code creatively shackled American film-makers well into the sixties.

Sticking to the Code

The infamous Production Code of 1930 comprised 13 subjects of regulation, including Crime, Sex, Vulgarity, Religion, Costume and National Feelings. Not all of it was absurd but much of it was. Themes that are accepted as normal in today's cinema were absolutely taboo. There was to be no nakedness, no passionate love scenes; 'impure love' such as adultery was not to be made appealing or be the subject of comedy. Crime could not be seen to pay and those who indulged in gambling or any other vice had to either see the light or come to a sticky end. Public officials could not be ridiculed and vulgar gestures and any semblance of bad language were outlawed. Just run that short list of restrictions against any number of modern movies and you can see how severely reigned-in were the film-makers of the time.

Movie scripts had to be cleared in advance by the regulators of the Code, who would demand all manner of cuts, some of them patently ridiculous. In the draft script for an early Otto Preminger film, for example, the director was requested to drop the customary kiss on both cheeks between two Frenchmen on the grounds that it might suggest homosexuality. To eliminate profanity, screenwriters were helpfully given a list of 28 prohibited words that included 'gawd', 'whore', 'damn' and 'hot' (in reference to a woman). Even William Shakespeare was not above censure, as Laurence Olivier discovered when he embarked on his 1944 production of *Henry V*. The word 'bastard', legitimately used by the Bard to describe someone born out of wedlock, was blue-pencilled by the censor.

The Production Code remained in place for 36 years, though there was some relaxation as time went on. Occasionally a film-maker would manage to get something past the censor. In Alfred Hitchcock's 1946 thriller *Notorious*, Cary Grant and Ingrid Bergman are locked into a two-and-a-half-minute kiss, vastly exceeding the three-second maximum permitted by the Code. The canny director achieved this by having his loving couple pause every few seconds before swiftly re-engaging, so that the overall effect is of a continuous bout.

Talking pictures

The Jazz Singer, starring Al Jolson, was premiered in New York on 6 October 1927. Made by Warner Brothers, it was the first full-length feature film to contain synchronised dialogue, though much of the movie was silent. Audiences also heard the star of the film sing three songs. It was enough to herald the end of the silent era.

For the studio, which had been going through tough times, it was more than a lifeline. It turned their fortunes around. Staking everything on the Vitaphone sound-on-disc system, one of several that had been developed in the rush to create talking pictures, they had stolen a march on their competitors (with the Vitaphone process the soundtrack was not printed on the film but recorded at 33 1/3rpm onto a series of discs that were played on a turntable attached to the projector while the movie was in progress). Sadly none of the four fraternal Warners was there to witness their triumph. The day before the premiere Sam Warner died of pneumonia and his three brothers hastened back to LA for the funeral.

The transition from silent movies to talkies was a gradual affair that took place over a number of years. None of the numerous competing technologies was perfect. Recording discs were fragile, cumbersome and unusable after 20 or so screenings. Actors (along with directors and technicians) had to learn new skills, always assuming they had acceptable voices – and by no means all of them did. And to complicate matters further, few cinemas had adequate sound facilities.

Some films, like *The Jazz Singer*, were half-talkie, half-silent. Other hybrids had some sound effects and music, but no audible speech. Nevertheless, by the end of the twenties it was clear to even the most diehard sceptic that talking pictures were here to stay. A cinema billboard of the time captured the mood:

PAUL MUNI IN 'SEVEN FACES' – ALL TALKING!

Breaking the silence

The 1928 Paramount movie The Shopworn Angel, *starring Gary Cooper and Nancy Carroll, aimed to cash in on the new craze for sound. A naive young soldier about to go off to war is taken up by a hard-boiled showgirl, a dalliance that leads to true love. Nancy Carroll can be heard singing the film's theme song over the opening credits and there are sound effects throughout the remaining 80 minutes, but there is no spoken dialogue until the closing moments of the movie. In the final scene, where the two lovers get married, the film's co-stars can be heard for the first time, uttering just two words apiece – and the same two words at that:*

'I do.'

Timeline to the talkies

1834 British mathematician William George Horner invents the zoetrope.

1878 Pioneering English photographer Eadweard Muybridge captures images of animals and people in motion.

1885 American manufacturer George Eastman produces flexible transparent film, key to the development of motion pictures.

1894 Thomas Alva Edison's kinetoscope is unveiled to the public.

1895 The Lumière brothers screen ten short films in Paris on their cinematograph.

1902 *Le voyage dans la lune* (*The Trip to the Moon*) (Georges Méliès).

1903 *The Great Train Robbery* (Edwin S. Porter).

1905 The nickelodeon in Pittsburgh is the first establishment devoted to showing motion pictures.

1909 Hollywood's first studio is built.

1911 Credits appear at the start of movies for the first time.

1914   Charlie Chaplin introduces his character of the Little Tramp.

1915   Carl Laemmle's Universal Studios is the first of the major companies to set up in Hollywood.

The Birth of a Nation (D. W. Griffith).

1919   Hollywood stars Douglas Fairbanks, Mary Pickford, Charlie Chaplin and D. W. Griffith found their own studio – United Artists.

1921   *The Sheik* establishes Rudolph Valentino as the screen's greatest lover.

1922   Alfred Hitchcock's first film as a director, *Number 13*, is never completed, as the funding dries up.

1923   A German shepherd, Rin Tin Tin, becomes cinema's first canine star.

Walt Disney Company is formed.

1925   *The Battleship Potemkin* (Sergei Eisenstein).

1927   *The Jazz Singer*, starring Al Jolson, is the first feature-length talkie.

CHAPTER 2

MOGUL EMPIRES

I hope I didn't make a mistake coming out here.
CARL LAEMMLE (FOUNDER OF UNIVERSAL STUDIOS)

By the 1920s the movie business was America's fourth largest. The industry was controlled by a handful of corporations that not only made the films but also distributed and exhibited them in their own cinema chains throughout the USA and overseas. In charge of these organisations, was a group of remarkable men: the Hollywood moguls.

The qualifications they brought to the job would hardly pass muster today. Most of them were Jewish immigrants, or sons of immigrants, from central and eastern Europe, with little or no formal education and only a slender grasp of the English language. As with many immigrant families, most changed or anglicised their names.

Humble beginnings

Before ending up in the entertainment business and becoming immensely rich, the moguls had all worked at menial jobs, often leading a hand-to-mouth existence.

Russian-born Louis B. Mayer, now of MGM (Metro–Goldwyn–Mayer) fame, joined his father as a scrap collector at the age of eight. Carl Laemmle, founder of Universal Studios, was a German immigrant who worked as a clerk in the garment and jewellery trades. Sam Goldwyn (originally Gelbfisz, then Goldfish) was born in Warsaw and became an apprentice in a glove factory. William Fox and Adolph Zukor both came from Hungary: Fox (aka Wilhelm Fried) began his working life in the garment industry; Zukor, head of Paramount, had been apprenticed to a furrier. The four Warner brothers, sons of a Polish cobbler who had 'adjusted' the family name of Wonskolaser, graduated from selling ice cream and soap to running a bicycle shop. Harry Cohn, who started Columbia Pictures with his brother Jack, was the son of German immigrants and a one-time pool hustler and song plugger.

Determined, resourceful and industrious, they were driven by a fierce desire to improve their lot. Penny arcades and nickelodeons were their passport to the world of entertainment but for them it was business, not pleasure. Mayer, the ex-junk dealer, bought his first modest picture house in Massachusetts in 1907 and built up a cinema chain that extended across several states and into Canada. He graduated to film production in 1918, hiring a studio in Brooklyn, before moving to Los Angeles. Zukor owned penny arcades before purchasing his first cinema in 1904. He imported European films – such as the Sarah Bernhardt classic *Queen Elizabeth* (1912) – to show in it (and other cinemas) before embarking on movie production himself, followed by the inevitable shift to Hollywood. Fox followed a similar route from penny arcade to cinema chain, then in 1912 began producing his own one-reelers, based on stories 'lifted' from women's magazines by his wife. Laemmle started in 1906 with a nickelodeon business in Chicago, which expanded into a chain of cinemas and a film distribution company, before he too was lured into production. The four Warner brothers owned a cinema in Pennsylvania and a movie distribution business in Pittsburgh before heading for California.

Sam Goldwyn and Harry Cohn might be said to have had a softer introduction to the movie business. Goldwyn abandoned the glove trade to join his brother-in-law Jesse Lasky and Cecil B. DeMille in their new production company, while Cohn learned the ropes as Carl Laemmle's assistant. One by one, the empire-builders arrived.

Hollywood harpies

Louella Parsons was America's first movie columnist; her words were syndicated to more than 400 newspapers worldwide with a readership of over 20 million. Her weekly radio show reached millions more. Publicity was the fuel that drove the Hollywood bandwagon and Parsons was its premier source.

For ten years she had it all her own way. Then, alarmed by her power to make or break a movie, or wilfully to undermine a career, the studios decided to give her some competition. Cue 53-year-old Hedda Hopper, a sharp-tongued ex-actress with no previous journalistic experience. Hopper, however, proved to be just as vicious and manipulative as her competitor. For the next 20 years there was a spiteful rivalry between the two women as they vied for the title of 'Queen of Hollywood', each trying to scoop the other and both being nervously wooed by the studios.

In 1985, when both were safely dead, Hollywood plucked up the courage to make a film about them. The title said it all: *Malice in Wonderland*.

Basic instincts

Despite obvious disadvantages on the cultural front, the moguls presided over some of the greatest films ever made. Wielding almost absolute power over those who worked for them, whether or not they were stars, the studio bosses were ruthless, mean, devious, often corrupt and only occasionally generous. They took loyalty for granted and never forgot a grudge. They would bully or cajole, depending on the situation or on whom they had in front of them. Robert Taylor, a major star at MGM, once went to see Louis B. Mayer to demand a pay rise. (For a number of years in the thirties and forties, Mayer himself was the highest salary earner in America.) He left Mayer's office with tears in his eyes. When someone asked him if he had successfully negotiated more money, the actor replied no but he had gained a father.

Film-makers were often frustrated by their bosses' ignorance, interference, prejudice and narrow-mindedness. But the moguls would insist that they knew what the public wanted – and they were frequently right. Columbia's Harry Cohn put it more graphically: 'I always know when there's something wrong with a story – my butt begins to itch.'

Mogul snapshots

Harry Cohn

A serial womaniser who preyed on the young starlets who passed (literally) through his hands. His first wife failed to bear him any children, so Cohn offered a starlet under contract to Columbia $125,000 if she bore him a daughter – with a $50,000 bonus if she made it a son. When the young woman declined his offer, he fired her.

Jack Warner

The most prominent of the four brothers, was at the forefront of his company for almost 50 years, breaking the sound barrier with The Jazz Singer and finishing up with an eight-Oscar haul for the 1964 musical My Fair Lady. He had long-running battles with his stars over contracts, James Cagney, Olivia de Havilland and Humphrey Bogart among those rebelling against the onerous terms. On one occasion Bette Davis fled to England in order to sever her contract. Warner personally pursued her there and took her to court. The studio won the action and the actress was made to return to work.

Sam Goldwyn

Sam fell in and out of partnership with various other moguls before finally setting up his own company (Samuel Goldwyn Productions) in 1924, though his name remained a component of MGM. He became as famous for his malapropisms as for the many fine movies that were made under his banner, having as much command of the English language as Del Boy (of *Only Fools and Horses* fame) has of French. Once, when planning to film a Broadway play, he was warned that the central character was a 'lesbian'. 'Don't worry,' responded Goldwyn, 'we'll make her an American.'

Carl Laemmle

Pronounced *lem-lee*, founder of Universal Studios, was universally known as 'Uncle Carl', the avuncular tag owing as much to his paternalistic style as to the fact that at one time he had close to 70 of his relatives on the payroll. Laemmle, who was something of a hypochondriac, was in the habit of jotting down his thoughts on a notepad wherever he happened to be, leaving the cryptic comments for his secretary to decipher later. On one occasion she puzzled over an item which simply read: 'Fair: 10.30.' Unable to fathom its meaning she consulted Laemmle, who eventually remembered that it referred to a bowel movement the previous evening that had been only moderately successful.

William Fox

The oldest of 13 children from an impoverished background. A botched operation following a childhood injury had left him with a withered left arm, but he overcame the handicap to become a fiercely competitive one-armed golfer. The same ruthless determination drove him in business and helped him to establish the powerful Fox Film Corporation. One day a man whom he had just appointed as a top studio executive asked Fox's advice on how he could make his presence felt among the workforce. 'It's easy,' Fox told him, 'you just call everybody into your office, one by one, and fire them. After a day or two you can hire them back, one by one. That way they'll know who's the boss.'

Hollywood on Hollywood:
Ten of the Best (film/director)

Sunset Boulevard (1950) **Billy Wilder**

Singin' in the Rain (1952) **Gene Kelly/Stanley Donen**

The Bad and the Beautiful (1952) **Vincente Minnelli**

A Star is Born (1954) **George Cukor**

The Big Knife (1955) **Robert Aldrich**

Barton Fink (1991) **Joel and Ethan Coen**

The Player (1992) **Robert Altman**

Gods and Monsters (1998) **Bill Condon**

Mulholland Drive (2001) **David Lynch**

The Artist (2011) **Michel Hazanavicius**

Illegal protection

The bosses would go to almost any lengths to keep hold of their stars or to preserve their valuable image – even if it meant breaking the law. In 1932 the producer Paul Bern, second husband of MGM superstar Jean Harlow (the 'Blonde Bombshell'), committed suicide at the couple's home in Benedict Canyon. They had been married three months, with Harlow just 21 years of age (she was 16 when she married the first time).

A farewell note alongside Bern's naked body (he had shot himself) hinted at sexual incompatibility. Promptly on the scene, even before the police were summoned, was studio boss L. B. Mayer. He immediately pocketed the note – a key piece of evidence – on the grounds that it might in some way compromise his prize sex goddess. Later, and very reluctantly, he was persuaded to hand it over to the authorities by the studio's publicity chief, Howard Strickling, who could see a jail sentence looming for his boss and perhaps for himself as an accessory. Five years on even Louis Mayer could do nothing to save Jean Harlow (real name Harlean Harlow Carpenter), who at 26 tragically died of kidney failure.

British mogul

Alexander Korda was a Hungarian Jew, but unlike his Hollywood counterparts he was well educated and had directed films in both Europe and America before finally settling in Britain. In 1932 he founded London Films, with Big Ben as its on-screen logo. Over the next 20 years the company produced many distinguished films, including *The Private Life of Henry VIII* (1933) with an ebullient Charles Laughton in the title role, *The Thief of Bagdad* (1940), *The Third Man* (1949), *The Tales of Hoffman* (1951) and Laurence Olivier's *Richard III* (1955).

Korda's ambition was to create a British film industry that would rival Hollywood, and he launched a number of glittering productions, not all of which were commercially successful. His two brothers – Zoltan, who directed, and Vincent, an Academy Award-winning art director – creatively collaborated on many of them. A flamboyant character, at one time married to the actress Merle Oberon, Korda injected some much-needed colour into the UK movie scene.

Flour power

The most unlikely film mogul of all was J. Arthur Rank. A millionaire flour miller and devout Methodist who came from Yorkshire, his initial interest in film was as a medium for promoting his religious beliefs. He built Pinewood Studios and bought the Odeon cinema chain from Oscar Deutsch (an ancient Greek word for a type of theatre, ODEON also served as an acronym for 'Oscar Deutsch Entertains Our Nation'). Rank later acquired the extensive studios at Denham and Ealing.

The Rank Organisation helped launch the careers of several important British directors, including David Lean, Carol Reed and Michael Powell, and via the so-called 'Rank Charm School' put stars like Dirk Bogarde, Diana Dors, Norman Wisdom and Christopher Lee on the road to fame. The organisation fell on hard times when it overreached itself in America and was forced to shed some of its studio assets, but the charitable and self-effacing J. Arthur Rank still managed to give away £100 million to Methodist causes during his lifetime.

Beating the gong

The trademark striking of a gong by a scantily clad, muscular man that introduces every Rank film first appeared in the mid-thirties. A number of suitably endowed figures have played the part, the most famous of them the ex-British heavyweight-boxing champion 'Bombardier' Billy Wells. His double striking of the gong resonates across dozens of films, but is not all it appears to be. The gong itself was made of plaster and papier mâché and the reverberating sound was added afterwards, but at least the muscles are real.

Ten mega box office flops

Film net loss (inflation adjusted)

Cutthroat Island (1995)

$147.2 million
(£92.7 million)

Director: Renny Harlin
Starring: Geena Davis, Matthew Modine

The Alamo (2004)

Director: John Lee Hancock
Starring: Dennis Quaid, Billy Bob Thornton

$146.6 million
(£92 million)

The Adventures of Pluto Nash (2002)

$145.9 million
(£91.8 million)

Director: Ron Underwood
Starring: Eddie Murphy, Randy Quaid

Sahara (2005)

Director: Breck Eisner
Starring: Matthew McConaughey,
Penélope Cruz

$144.9 million
(£91 million)

Mars Needs Moms (2011)

$140.5 million
(£88.5 million)

Director: Simon Wells
Starring: Seth Green, Joan Cusack

The 13th Warrior (1999)
Director: John McTiernan
Starring: Antonio Banderas

$137.1 million
(£86 million)

Town and Country (2001)
Director: Peter Chelsom
Starring: Warren Beatty, Diane Keaton,
Goldie Hawn

$124.2 million
(£78 million)

Speed Racer (2008)
Director: Andy/Lana Wachowski
Starring: Emile Hirsch, Christina Ricci

$114.5 million
(£72 million)

Heaven's Gate (1980)
Director: Michael Cimino
Starring: Kris Kristofferson, Christopher Walken

$114.3 million
(£72 million)

Stealth (2005)
Director: Rob Cohen
Starring: Jamie Foxx

$111.7 million
(£70 million)

Studio system

In their heyday, which began in the 1920s and lasted for nearly 40 years, the studios were run like individual townships. Each had its own contracted actors, directors, producers, writers, cinematographers, designers and composers, plus a large workforce that included just about every job description from clerk to chauffeur, carpenter to cook. Each studio had its own police and fire departments, medical facilities and a school for child actors to attend when they weren't on the set. With the bigger studios turning out 40-50 films a year there was plenty of work to go round, with the working day starting at 7 a.m., six days a week.

Each studio's principal asset was its stars who were pampered and protected (but also frequently bullied) by the moguls, who in effect owned them and tried with varying degrees of success to control every aspect of their lives. In return for the material benefits of stardom (not to mention the boost to the ego), actors were expected to fulfil their contracts, often lasting for seven years or more, to the letter. Dissent was not tolerated: you took the roles which were assigned to you. Actors who didn't toe the line could be suspended without pay or humiliatingly loaned out to other studios, or worse, fired. Some major stars struggled to break free from the studio system (Cary Grant was one of the first to succeed) but most settled for their lot.

CHAPTER 3

MADE IN BRITAIN

There is a real revival in the British film industry, but there is a danger that we will become colonial servants of Hollywood.

MIKE LEIGH, DIRECTOR

The British film industry made a sluggish start. There was no D. W. Griffith or Sergei Eisenstein to lead the way. No Charlie Chaplin to illuminate the path with his comic genius (even though he had been British-born). There was no shortage of people turning a camera, but the quality and range of the movies fell far behind those produced on the other side of the Atlantic. The UK climate was not conducive to outdoor filming and there was a lack of entrepreneurial flair. The most popular early films were crudely truncated versions of Shakespeare and Victorian literary classics.

Alfred Hitchcock was the first director to make an impact. He had started his film career designing titles for silent movies, but swiftly moved on to directing. His 1926 thriller *The Lodger*, based on a Jack-the-Ripper-style novel by Marie Belloc Lowndes, was a critical and box-office success. Three years later he made the UK's first 'talkie', *Blackmail*. Some of the tension-building techniques that became hallmarks of Hitchcock's later films were developed during this period.

Movie howler

Van Johnson plays a blind American playwright in the 1956 thriller 23 Paces to Baker Street. His rented apartment in Portman Square, just 23 short steps from one of London's most famous thoroughfares, has a balcony overhanging the Thames – a blind spot on the part of the film's producers since Portman Square is actually a good two miles from the river.

Coming of age

The 1930s saw the British film industry make great strides forward. The producer/director Alexander Korda founded London Films and embarked on a series of major productions including *The Scarlet Pimpernel* (1934), with Leslie Howard in the title role, and the futuristic *Things to Come* (1936), based on an H. G. Wells novel. Hitchcock delivered three of his finest films on the trot: *The Man Who Knew Too Much* (1934), starring the Slovakian-born Peter Lorre and infinitely better than the director's 1956 remake with James Stewart and Doris Day, *The 39 Steps* (1935), with Robert Donat as Richard Hannay, and *The Lady Vanishes* (1938), with Margaret Lockwood and Michael Redgrave heading a strong cast.

Waiting in the wings were three more young film-makers who would establish international reputations: David Lean, Carol Reed and Michael Powell.

David Lean

The wartime naval drama *In Which We Serve* (1941) gave David Lean his first directorial credit. He co-directed the film (Lean was responsible for the action sequences) with Noël Coward, who also wrote the screenplay and the music and played the leading role. The movie was a great morale-booster for the blitzed British public, though it appears somewhat dated now. Over the next few years Lean made one great film after another, including the achingly romantic *Brief Encounter* (1945) and two magnificent adaptations of Charles Dickens novels, *Great Expectations* (1946) and *Oliver Twist* (1948). In the mid-1950s he changed gear, opting to make movies on an epic scale. *The Bridge on the River Kwai* (1957) and *Lawrence of Arabia* (1962) won him Oscars and he had further spectacular success with *Doctor Zhivago* in 1965. His last film, *A Passage to India* (1984), was somewhat marred by the miscasting of Alec Guinness, a David Lean 'regular', as the Indian professor Godbole.

Carol Reed

An illegitimate son of the famous Edwardian actor–manager Sir Herbert Beerbohm Tree, Carol Reed grew up with theatre in his blood. He started out as a stage actor and made the move into film as a dialogue coach at Ealing Studios. Reed's finest work (despite his Oscar for *Oliver!* 20 years later) came in the 1940s, with movies like *Odd Man Out* (1946), *The Fallen Idol* (1948) and, most famously, *The Third Man* (1949) with its shadowy scenes of war-torn Vienna and the haunting zither music of Anton Karas – not to mention Orson Welles as the disarmingly evil Harry Lime. Reed made the last two of these films in collaboration with the writer Graham Greene and later directed the movie version of Greene's novel *Our Man in Havana* (1959).

Michael Powell

Michael Powell and his Hungarian partner Emeric Pressburger (their production company was called 'The Archers') made some of the most original films in British cinema. The division of labour varied from film to film, though Powell did most of the directing, with the screenplays generally a combined effort. Among their most successful films (creatively, if not at the box office) are *The Life and Death of Colonel Blimp* (1943), *A Matter of Life and Death* (1946), *Black Narcissus* (1946) and *The Red Shoes* (1948). In 1960 as a solo effort, Powell made *Peeping Tom*, a movie about a voyeuristic killer who films his victims in their death throes. The subject matter horrified the critics and damaged the director's reputation. *Peeping Tom* is now a highly regarded film, though its redemption came too late for Michael Powell, who died in 1990 before the critical tide had turned.

Ealing comedies

For ten years after World War Two, Ealing Studios in West London became the Mecca of British film comedy. Under the supervision of production chief Michael Balcon, a group of talented directors churned out a series of classic comedies that are still popular today. Among the first off the production line were *Passport to Pimlico* and *Whisky Galore*, both released in 1949.

The Ealing films provided steady work for a number of British character actors, who cropped up in one picture after another. They also revealed the comic talents of Alec Guinness, who starred in several of them: *Kind Hearts and Coronets* (1949), in which he plays eight different members of the same family, all of whom are cheerfully murdered by a dishonoured relative; *The Lavender Hill Mob* and *The Man in the White Suit* (both 1951) and *The Ladykillers* (1955), about the antics of an inept criminal gang. The Coen Brothers remade the latter in 2004, with Tom Hanks in the Alec Guinness role, but it only served to show how much better the original was.

New wave

Britain's working class became the focus of a new wave of film-makers in the late fifties and early sixties, with dynamic young actors like Albert Finney, Tom Courtenay and Richard Harris becoming stars overnight. Most of the films were adaptations of contemporary novels or stage plays, broadly categorised as 'kitchen sink' dramas. They established the reputations of several directors who would become major figures in British cinema: Tony Richardson (*Look Back in Anger*, 1959), Karel Reisz (*Saturday Night and Sunday Morning*, 1960), Lindsay Anderson (*This Sporting Life*, 1962) and John Schlesinger (*A Kind of Loving*, 1962).

As the decade moved on, social realism gave way to the more upbeat mood of the 'swinging sixties'. The first Bond movie, *Dr. No*, hit the screens in 1962, and three years later the bespectacled spy Harry Palmer (Michael Caine) made his first appearance in *The Ipcress File*. British cinema was going up in size, too, with David Lean's epic *Lawrence of Arabia* followed by two other historical blockbusters, the eighteenth-century romp *Tom Jones* (1963) and the Tudor tragedy *A Man for All Seasons* (1966), each picking up a handful of Oscars. Two American émigrés – Joseph Losey and Stanley Kubrick – anchored themselves in the UK and produced some influential films. Losey made three critically acclaimed movies in tandem with the playwright Harold Pinter (*The Servant*, 1963; *Accident*, 1967; and *The Go-Between*, 1971), each exploring the politics of sexuality, gender and class in British society. Kubrick helped energise the UK film industry with three groundbreaking movies: the Cold War comedy *Dr. Strangelove* (1963), the enigmatic sci-fi epic *2001: A Space Odyssey* (1968) and the exceedingly violent *A Clockwork Orange* (1971) – so violent in fact that Kubrick withdrew the film in the UK on police advice and it remained under wraps for 27 years.

Eye opener

For the disturbing brainwashing sequence in Stanley Kubrick's 1971 film A Clockwork Orange, actor Malcolm McDowell, playing a punk sociopath, was required to have his eyes propped open for long periods of time by means of a medical device called a 'lid lock'. The scene was successfully shot but the actor suffered a scratched cornea and temporary blindness.

Staying home

The movie industry is a truly international business, with a cross-pollination of talent – actors, writers, directors and technicians – that often blurs the national provenance of a film. It doesn't help that independent film-makers typically obtain their financial backing from a variety of sources, leaving a confusing paper trail as to the ownership of the movie. Several British directors like Alan Parker, Ridley Scott, Stephen Daldry and Sam Mendes have criss-crossed the pond. But two of the UK's most acclaimed film-makers have, for the most part, elected to work at home.

Ken Loach

Ken Loach cut his teeth directing episodes of *Z-Cars* on television. His first feature film, *Poor Cow*, was made in 1967 but it was his second picture *Kes* (1969), about a young boy and his kestrel, which struck a chord with critics and the public alike. Loach's films reflect his strong left-wing views and often take on an anti-establishment stance, but whatever their bias (or the viewer's own political sympathies) there is no denying the quality of the acting performances he elicits (often from non-professionals) or the compelling nature of the stories he tells. His films have won several major awards, including the coveted Palme d'Or at Cannes for *The Wind that Shakes the Barley* (2006).

Mike Leigh

In Mike Leigh's films the generally depressing lives of his characters are conveyed with disturbing realism, only occasionally leavened by humour. Between his first picture in 1971 (appropriately titled *Bleak Moments*) and his second there was a 17-year gap, during which Leigh honed his style, often involving improvisation by the actors, in a series of notable television plays. Two films that broke the mould are *Topsy-Turvy* (1999), about the musical duo Gilbert and Sullivan, and *Mr. Turner* (2014), which has a curmudgeonly performance from Timothy Spall as the eccentric British painter. Among Leigh's many awards are the Cannes Film Festival's Palme d'Or for *Secrets & Lies* (1996) and Venice's 'Golden Lion' for *Vera* (2004).

Harry Potter movies: crunching the numbers

 25,000 *items of clothing were made for the series.*

 160 *pairs of spectacles were used by Daniel Radcliffe as Harry Potter, many of them without glass to avoid reflecting the cameras.*

 900 *hand-labelled Memory Vials are housed in the cabinet in Dumbledore's office.*

 39-*year-old actress Shirley Henderson – Moaning Myrtle in* Harry Potter and the Chamber of Secrets *(2002) and* Harry Potter and the Goblet of Fire *(2005) – was the oldest to play a Hogwarts student.*

 3,800 *stunt performers and film doubles were used across the eight movies.*

 588 *individual film sets were created for the series.*

 4,500 *giant scallop shells made up the roof of Shell Cottage.*

 210,000 *coins were manufactured for the Gringotts Bank scenes.*

$1.155 billion (£716.1 million) *was the total production budget for the series.*

 19 hours 39 minutes *is how long it would take to watch all eight movies back to back.*

A woman's touch

For its first hundred years the British film industry was overwhelmingly a man's world – that is, behind the camera. Aside from the tasks and roles routinely performed by women, such as make-up, continuity and production assistant, there was a marked lack of female input, except perhaps as a screenwriter. Jill Craigie, wife of the Labour politician Michael Foot, made a number of distinguished documentaries in the thirties and a solitary feature film, *Blue Scar*, in 1949. Muriel Box (who, with her husband the writer–producer Sydney Box, won an Oscar for the screenplay of *The Seventh Veil* (1945), starring James Mason and Ann Todd) went on to direct a dozen or so undistinguished films in the 1950s and early sixties. But these were the exceptions rather than the norm.

It wasn't until the 1990s that female directors began to make their mark, with films like Sally Potter's *Orlando* (1992), based on the Virginia Woolf novel, Gurinder Chadha's humorously sensitive portrait of British Asian women, *Bhaji on the Beach* (1993) and Carine Adler's painful study of a 19-year-old's psychological breakdown, *Under the Skin* (1997), which gave Samantha Morton her first starring role. Since then, more and more female writers and directors have entered the fray. Leading the charge are Phyllida Law (*Mamma Mia!*, 2008), Andrea Arnold (*Fish Tank*, 2009), Lynne Ramsay (*We Need to Talk About Kevin*, 2011) and Sam Taylor-Johnson (*Fifty Shades of Grey*, 2015).

Waving the flag

Two men were largely responsible for keeping British cinema afloat during the lean years of the seventies and eighties: actor-turned-director Richard Attenborough and producer David Puttnam (both later elevated to the peerage). Attenborough campaigned tirelessly for the industry and eventually persuaded the UK government to direct some of the National Lottery money its way. An equally committed David Puttnam helped launch the careers of young British directors like Alan Parker, Hugh Hudson and Roland Joffé, before setting off for Hollywood as CEO of Columbia Pictures.

In recent years UK film-makers have produced a string of international hits, from Stephen Frears' *The Queen* (2006) to Danny Boyle's *Slumdog Millionaire* (2008) and from Joe Wright's *Atonement* (2007) to Tom Hooper's *The King's Speech* (2010).

The UK's comprehensive studio facilities, technical prowess (not least in the special-effects department) and tax incentives have encouraged many top American directors to film here, among them the heavyweight trio of Martin Scorsese, Steven Spielberg and George Lucas; to all of which can be added the eight Harry Potter films and 50 years of James Bond. No longer in the shadow of Hollywood, British cinema is spending some time in the sun.

The Seven Ages of 007

Seven actors have played James Bond on film if the 1967 spoof version of *Casino Royale* is included. Each actor was a different age when he made his debut in the role.

In order of appearance:

	Actor	Debut film	Age
	Sean Connery	*Dr. No* (1962)	32
	David Niven	*Casino Royale* (1967)	57
	George Lazenby	*On Her Majesty's Secret Service* (1969)	30
	Roger Moore	*Live and Let Die* (1973)	46
	Timothy Dalton	*The Living Daylights* (1987)	41
	Pierce Brosnan	*GoldenEye* (1995)	42
	Daniel Craig	*Casino Royale* (2006)	38

CHAPTER 4

MAKE 'EM LAUGH!

All I need to make a comedy is a park, a policeman and a pretty girl.
CHARLES CHAPLIN

'Make 'em laugh!' sings Donald O'Connor in his acrobatically funny song-and-dance routine in the classic musical *Singin' in the Rain*. Comedy is one of cinema's oldest genres, dating back to the peep-show slapstick routines that entertained the wide-eyed viewers of the kinetoscope. In the absence of dialogue the humour of the silent era was strictly visual, relying heavily on pile-ups and pratfalls, on colliding characters and custard-pie fights.

With the arrival of sound the emphasis switched to verbal humour, wordplay taking over from the exclusive diet of physical comedy. This was particularly evident in an entirely new brand of humour that emerged from Hollywood in the early 1930s. Screwball comedy was a scatty blend of slapstick and sophistication, characterised by razor-sharp, fast-paced dialogue. The genre proved very popular during the years of the Great Depression and often light-heartedly depicts the social classes in conflict, with the underprivileged generally coming out on top (unlike in real life) – as in *My Man Godfrey* (1936), starring William Powell and Carole Lombard. Screwball comedies frequently feature befuddled heroes and assertive heroines who are romantically entwined before the closing credits, e.g. Cary Grant and Katharine Hepburn in Howard Hawks's *Bringing Up Baby* (1938) or Henry Fonda and Barbara Stanwyck in Preston Sturges's *The Lady Eve* (1941). By the end of the forties the genre had petered out, though elements of it surfaced in other comedy styles.

As writers assumed a more creatively significant role, so the range of screen comedy expanded, reflecting the conventions and preoccupations of the times. Iconic movies from each of the main comedy categories include: Charlie Chaplin's *The Great Dictator*, 1940 (satirical), Peter Sellers in *Dr. Strangelove or: How I Learned to Stop Worrying and Love the Bomb*, 1963 (black), *Monty Python's Life of Brian*, 1979 (anarchic), Billy Crystal and Meg Ryan in *When Harry Met Sally*, 1989 (romantic) and Mike Myers in *Austin Powers in Goldmember*, 2002 (spoof). In short, anything for a laugh!

Taking the Charlie

The highest number of takes on record for a single scene is 324, clocked by perfectionist Charlie Chaplin during the making of his 1931 film City Lights.

Keystone comedy

The master of the earlier style of slapstick comedy was Mack Sennett, a Canadian-born actor–director who founded the Keystone Studios in Hollywood in 1912. Over the next 23 years Sennett made hundreds of frenetically paced short films, most of them silent. He worked with the best comedic talent of the time – Roscoe 'Fatty' Arbuckle, Harold Lloyd, Buster Keaton and W. C. Fields were just some of those who came under his direction. Charlie Chaplin made his screen debut in a Keystone film in 1914, and went on to create his signature tramp character there. Many of Sennett's earlier films featured the Keystone Cops (originally 'Kops'), a hopelessly incompetent collection of truncheon-wielding policemen, hugely popular with cinema audiences who loved seeing the forces of law and order lampooned.

Kings of comedy

The silent era's undisputed 'kings of comedy' were Harold Lloyd, Buster Keaton and Charlie Chaplin.

Harold Lloyd

Harold Lloyd's most distinctive feature was his outsized horn-rimmed glasses, a prop he adopted for his on-screen persona of a mild-mannered young man whose determination to make his way in the world is constantly thwarted by formidable obstacles. He did most of the physical stunts in his films himself, some of them at high-level despite the fact that he had no head for heights. The most famous of these comes in the aptly titled *Safety Last* (1923), where he hangs from a clock face high above a busy street. He was the highest paid comedy star of the 1920s, and many would say he deserved every cent.

Buster Keaton

Buster Keaton joined his parents' vaudeville act at the age of three. As part of their comedy routine he would be tossed around on stage, and sometimes into the audience. He learned to keep a straight face, which became his trademark as his on-screen character stoically suffered mishap after mishap, a serial victim of misfortune and misunderstanding – and, very often, machinery. Many of his films, over which he came to have full artistic control, are comedy classics, among them *The Navigator* (1924), *Sherlock, Jr.* (1924) and *The General* (1926). Alcoholism shortened his career, though he later played cameos in other people's films, among them Billy Wilder's look back to the silent era, *Sunset Boulevard* (1950).

Charlie Chaplin

Charlie Chaplin's movie career spanned 52 years. He was a one-man band; the director, producer and editor of his films as well as the star. He created the storylines and composed the music. Combining slapstick with pathos, he switched his audience from laughter to tears as if turning on a tap. The Little Tramp's bowler hat, cane and moustache became symbols of a universal folk hero, the shabby costume cloaking an elegance of spirit. The audience never heard the character speak – they didn't need to. In one of Chaplin's last films, *Limelight*, a talkie made in 1952, he and Buster Keaton performed together for the only time. In an uproariously funny on-stage routine, without dialogue, the two aging comic geniuses show why they will never be forgotten.

Fall guy

It was the great magician Houdini who gave Joseph Frank Keaton the nickname 'Buster'. While on tour with the Keaton family, Houdini had seen the young Joseph take a tumble down a long flight of stairs and survive unscathed. He described the fall as a 'real buster' (in the parlance of the time, a potentially damaging spill) and the sobriquet caught on.

Juggling with names

The misanthropic W. C. Fields, with his bulbous nose and unpadded paunch, was 36 when he made his first movie, *Pool Sharks*, in 1915. He was already an international vaudeville star, a juggler who had performed at the Folies Bergère in Paris and, by royal command, at Buckingham Palace. He effortlessly made the transition from silent films to talkies, his adenoidal drawl and richly comic turn of phrase fleshing out his screen character, with its deep-rooted suspicion of women, children and animals.

'W. C. Fields' was a condensed version of his real name, William Claude Dukenfield, but the pseudonyms didn't stop there. Fields wrote or co-wrote most of his movies, his contribution thinly disguised by some exotic nomenclature. His writing credit for *It's a Gift* (1934) is 'Charles Bogle' (Fields insisting it sounded like 'Bo' not 'Bog')', for *The Bank Dick* (1940) it is 'Mahatma Kane Jeeves' and for *Never Give a Sucker an Even Break* (1941), 'Otis Criblecoblis'. The actor was notoriously thrifty and in his vaudeville days had adopted the habit of opening bank accounts wherever he toured. Among the names under which he registered them were Aristotle Hoop, Sneed Hearn, Figley E. Whitesides and Ludovic Fishpond. Since he failed to keep track of the accounts, only a few of the several hundred he opened could be traced after his death.

And then there were three

Like many of their Hollywood contemporaries, the Marx Brothers began their careers in vaudeville. There were five of them in the act (in descending order of age): Chico (Leonard), Harpo (Adolph/Arthur), Groucho (Julius), Gummo (Milton) and Zeppo (Herbert). According to Groucho Marx, Chico's nickname stemmed from his penchant for young women (in those days referred to as 'chicks'), Harpo played the harp, Gummo's favourite footwear was the gumshoe, Zeppo was named after the recently invented zepplin and Groucho was so-called because of his disgruntled nature.

Gummo was the first to go, dropping out of the act before the brothers were signed up for their first movie in 1921 (entitled *Humor Risk*, it was never released). Their second film, eight years later, was a musical comedy, *The Cocoanuts*, followed by an even bigger hit the following year, *Animal Crackers*. After three more box-office successes in consecutive years – *Monkey Business* (1931), *Horse Feathers* (1932) and *Duck Soup* (1933) – Zeppo left to join Gummo in his theatrical agency and developed a very profitable third career running an engineering company.

The remaining three Marx brothers – Groucho, Harpo and Chico – made eight more films together, the best of which are *A Night at the Opera* (1935), *A Day at the Races* (1937) and *A Night in Casablanca* (1946).

Hardy minus Laurel

Stan Laurel and Oliver Hardy made 106 films together in their 19-year screen partnership, and only once in that time did either one of them star in a film with anyone else. It happened in 1939 when Laurel walked out of the studio following a contractual spat. In the film, Zenobia, Hardy's sparring partner is the former silent-screen star Harry Langdon, who at the peak of his career ranked alongside Charlie Chaplin, Buster Keaton and Harold Lloyd. The film was not a great success and, happily for the millions of Laurel and Hardy fans, normal service was resumed soon afterwards.

High-octane performer

Nobody could have accused Jerry Lewis (real name Joseph Levitch) of not throwing himself into a part. In American cinema he is one in a distinguished line of put-upon individuals, but unlike some of his predecessors – the placid Stan Laurel or the phlegmatic Buster Keaton for example – Lewis's response to the intractable obstacles that confront him borders on the hysterical. His eyes cross, his body goes into spasms and his tongue becomes tied in knots.

Between 1949 and 1956 he made 17 films with Dean Martin, his character's gormless antics contrasting with the handsome Martin's laconic detachment. When the pair split up, Lewis had a fruitful partnership with the director Frank Tashlin who helped him to develop his comedy as a solo artist. But most critics agree that Lewis's most inventive and satisfyingly funny material came in the half-dozen or so movies he co-wrote and directed himself during the sixties, starting with *The Bellboy* (1960). In *The Nutty Professor* (1963), his hilarious take on Dr Jekyll and Mr Hyde, Lewis plays not one but two parts – the nerdy, socially inadequate Professor Kelp and his serum-induced alter ego, the smooth-talking stud Buddy Love. It was Martin and Lewis in one.

Out of sight

One Jerry Lewis film has never been released. The Day the Clown Cried *(1972) tells the heart-rending story of a washed-up German circus clown who is incarcerated in a Nazi concentration camp for having drunkenly made fun of Adolf Hitler. Ridiculed and rejected by the other inmates in the camp, he finds an appreciative audience among the Jewish children there and eventually accompanies them to Auschwitz and the gas chambers. Lewis directed the film as well as playing the lead role, but legal wranglings with the writers and original backer of the movie have prevented it being shown. There has been much speculation as to how good or bad a film it is but one thing is certain – it is not like any other Jerry Lewis movie.*

Capitalist clown

Norman Wisdom was Britain's top comedy movie star of the fifties – and he was just as big in Albania, which at the time was a country cut off from almost everywhere else. The isolated Communist regime viewed Wisdom's screen character, Norman Pitkin (the little man always put-upon by authoritarian figures), as a hapless victim of the corrupt capitalist system. His movies were constantly shown in cinemas and on TV, and he is still revered there today even though Albania's political stance has changed.

Clues to Clouseau

Peter Ustinov was scheduled to play Chief Inspector Clouseau in the 1964 film *The Pink Panther*, but pulled out of the production at the last minute. His replacement, Peter Sellers, was not as well known internationally – or at all to the director Blake Edwards, who met the actor for the first time when he arrived in Rome to begin shooting. The principal star of the film was David Niven (playing the urbane Sir Charles Lytton), who was hoping that it would provide a much-needed boost to his career. In the event, it was Sellers who stole the picture.

Sellers brought the full range of his comedic skills to the character of the accident-prone French policeman. Central to his interpretation of Clouseau was his appearance, which was sparked by a box of matches, the trademark of which featured an image of Captain Matthew Webb, who in 1875 had become the first man to swim the English Channel. Webb's chiselled features and heroically bristling moustache were the key to Clouseau's fastidious vanity and idiotic pride. The familiar hat and trench coat were also the actor's idea. A superb mimic, Sellers had created dozens of character voices in his time, but none more distinctive than Clouseau's. The ultimate joke is that the policeman's accent is so distorted that even his fellow countrymen have difficulty understanding him. It is a measure of Sellers' comic creation that actors as accomplished as Alan Arkin and Steve Martin, both of whom have had turns as Clouseau, pale into insignificance alongside the uniquely funny original.

Comedy connection

The American television show *Saturday Night Live* has been a nursery for comedy talent since it was first transmitted in 1975, with many of its performers going on to successful careers in the movies.

Among the first to make it onto the big screen was John Belushi, who starred in the 1978 anarchic comedy hit *National Lampoon's Animal House*. Two years later fellow *SNL* cast member Dan Aykroyd teamed up with him in *The Blues Brothers*, which began life as one of their TV sketches. Chevy Chase had a major success in *National Lampoon's Vacation* (1985), and went on to star in three sequels. Bill Murray, Billy Crystal and Eddie Murphy joined the list of those who upgraded to film, Murphy becoming one of Hollywood's biggest comedy stars with movies like *Beverly Hills Cop* (1984), *Coming to America* (1988) and *The Nutty Professor* (1996). The one and only Robin Williams was another *SNL* regular who built a stellar film career, though he saved his most rampantly funny performances for TV and stand-up.

Mike Myers' feature-film debut was in *Wayne's World* (1992), adapted from a *Saturday Night Live* sketch. Five years later he had an even bigger success with the introduction of his buck-toothed, spy-about-town, *Austin Powers: International Man of Mystery*. Adam Sandler and Will Ferrell are two other veterans of the long-running TV show who have put their stamp on film comedy. They are unlikely to be the last. .

Carry On carrying on

There were 30 *Carry On* films in all, starting with *Carry on Sergeant* in 1958. The last in the series was *Carry on Columbus,* released in 1992. The director/producer team of Gerald Thomas and Peter Rogers was at the helm throughout.

Total number of appearances made by leading actors:

Kenneth Williams	26
Joan Sims	24
Charles Hawtrey	23
Sid James	19
Kenneth Connor	17
Peter Butterworth	16
Hattie Jacques	14
Bernard Breslaw	14
Jim Dale	11
Barbara Windsor	10
Jack Douglas	8
Terry Scott	7
Leslie Phillips	4*

*There was a 32-year gap between Leslie Phillips' third and fourth appearances.

CHAPTER 5

ALL SINGING,
ALL DANCING

He can give the audience pleasure just by walking across the floor.
GENE KELLY ABOUT FRED ASTAIRE

When Al Jolson got down on one knee in *The Jazz Singer* and audibly poured out his heart to 'Mammy', it was Hollywood's cue to usher in a new movie genre. The arrival of sound unleashed a flood of musicals, with every studio determined to capitalise on the novelty of song and dance on film. It was the era of the backstage musical with *The Broadway Melody* of 1929 ('100 per cent All Talking* All Singing* All Dancing*!') setting the pace. Unfortunately most of the movies that followed it were distinctly mediocre, if not downright bad, and within a few short years audiences were staying away from the endless procession of chorus lines with their high kicks and rictus smiles.

Dancing master

One film reversed the trend. The smash hit *42nd Street* (1933) was a familiar backstage story: an unknown face from the chorus replaces the indisposed star of a new Broadway musical on its opening night, becoming a star herself in the process. But what lifted the film head and shoulders above all the others, apart from its snappy dialogue and all-star cast, were the dazzling production numbers, created by one of cinema's greatest choreographers, Busby Berkeley.

It was the years of the Great Depression, and in film after film Busby Berkeley did his best to lift the national gloom by manoeuvring battalions of stunningly (and often scantily) costumed chorus girls into spectacular formations: kaleidoscopic shapes, floral patterns and on one occasion a gorgeously animated American flag. The camera was used to visually exciting effect, tracking through a tunnel of shapely legs or capturing the interlocking limbs from on high. In one memorable number girls dance in the dark while 'playing' violins outlined in neon – and all this from a man who had never had a dancing lesson in his life.

Fred and Ginger

Fred Astaire and Ginger Rogers made ten movies together. Only the last, *The Barkleys of Broadway* (1949), which reunited the pair after a ten-year gap, was in colour. Despite that, their films retain a freshness and vitality that shrugs off the fact that they were made three-quarters of a century ago. Astaire had more accomplished dancing partners – the balletic Cyd Charisse, for example, or Eleanor Powell, billed as 'The World's Greatest Tap Dancer' – but there was a chemistry between 'Fred and Ginger' that radiated on screen and enthralled cinema audiences around the world. In their first film together, *Flying Down to Rio* (1933), they were fourth and fifth billing, but one sensational dance number – 'The Carioca' – was enough to catapult them to stardom.

Astaire rejected Busby Berkeley's use of tricky camera angles, insisting that he should always be shot full length during a number and be viewed from the audience's perspective. He was a hard taskmaster, though very patient, and he and Ginger only had one serious falling out. It happened during the making of *Top Hat* (1935), their fourth film together. Ginger's eye-catching ostrich-feathered dress kept shedding its feathers while the couple were dancing, getting up Astaire's nose in more ways than one. She (and her mother, who remained the driving force behind her career) refused to substitute another costume. No lasting harm was done to the relationship, though from then on Ginger was known as 'Feathers'.

Wizard outfit

Actor Frank Morgan plays the title role in the MGM version of L. Frank Baum's classic tale The Wizard of Oz *(1939). To play the bogus wizard Morgan was kitted out in a vintage black cutaway coat with a velvet collar, which had been purchased from a second-hand store in Los Angeles by the studio's wardrobe department. One day on the set, when turning out the pockets, the actor discovered the name 'L. Frank Baum' inscribed on the lining. The studio tracked down the tailor in Chicago who confirmed that the coat had indeed been made for the author. Baum's widow also identified the garment. MGM strenuously denied that it was a publicity stunt – just a wizard coincidence then.*

MGM musicals

While the genre remained popular (and while there was sufficient money in the kitty) every studio made musicals, but for a period of 15 years after the end of World War Two, no one made them better than MGM. The studio had produced some notable musicals before this, not least *The Wizard of Oz* in 1939, but the post-war years brought together some of the finest talents of all time. There were stars like Judy Garland and Frank Sinatra, Cyd Charisse and Fred Astaire, Howard Keel and Jane Powell, top directors like Vincente Minnelli and Stanley Donen and composers and musicians like the precocious André Previn, who joined MGM as an arranger at the age of 15. There was no single blueprint of an MGM musical but what the very best of them had in common, over and above the star attractions, were an engaging storyline, memorable songs and some breathtaking dance routines – like choreographer Michael Kidd's dazzling barn-raising dance in *Seven Brides for Seven Brothers* (1954) – which made the films emerging from other studios seem positively static.

The man who inspirationally marshalled all this creative and performing talent was songwriter-turned-producer Arthur Freed, who wrote the lyrics for the songs in *Singin' in the Rain*. For 20 years Freed was in charge of the studio's musical output. It was on his watch, in 1942, that a young Broadway song-and-dance man made his screen debut in a film called *For Me and My Gal*. His name was Gene Kelly.

Gotta dance!

Gene Kelly is the one hoofer who can be mentioned in the same breath as Fred Astaire. But whereas the elegant Astaire is always graceful and sublimely smooth, Kelly's dancing style is robust and athletically inventive – in *Anchors Aweigh* (1945) he dances with an animated mouse (the idea was director Stanley Donen's) and in *It's Always Fair Weather* (1955) he does an ankle-threatening tap routine on roller skates.

Three iconic Gene Kelly movies came in the space of a few years: *On the Town* (1949), shot on the streets of New York to a pre-recorded soundtrack and the first musical to be filmed on location; *An American in Paris* (1951) with its 15-minute ballet sequence at the end of the movie (unlike the character he plays with his stumbling French, Kelly himself was a Francophile who spoke the language fluently); and *Singin' in the Rain* (1952), a glorious parody of the coming of sound – which is where it all began. Kelly made several films as a straight actor and directed others, but it is for his unique contribution to the Hollywood musical that he will best be remembered.

Musical mix

Broadway has been the source of many film musicals, from the 1920s Sigmund Romberg operetta *The Desert Song* (of which there have been three movie versions) to *Hairspray*, based on John Waters' cult comedy of the eighties. During the fifties and sixties the Rodgers and Hammerstein production line saw one hit show after another transfer to the big screen: *Oklahoma!* (1955), *Carousel* (1956), *The King and I* (1956), *South Pacific* (1958) and *The Sound of Music* (1965). The films were straightforward adaptations of the stage productions, often cumbersomely shot and propped up by their already popular songs. This now began to change. Driven by directorial trends elsewhere in the movies, musicals became more cinematic in style, whether they were based on Broadway shows or not – and with this shift in style came a marked change in subject matter.

West Side Story (1961), a reworking of Shakespeare's *Romeo and Juliet* with music by Leonard Bernstein (who had written the score for *On the Town*), is about the ethnic rivalry of New York's teenage street gangs. *Fiddler on the Roof* (1971) is set against the background of Tsarist Russian pogroms against the Jews, while *Cabaret* (1972), with groundbreaking choreography and direction from Bob Fosse, deals with the rise of Nazism in 1930s Berlin. It's all a long way from the innocent backstage storylines of the early screen musicals.

Initially a failure, *The Rocky Horror Picture Show* (1975), an outrageous send-up of sci-fi and horror movies with a transvestite transsexual from Transylvania as the central character, became a cult hit, especially among the gay community. Film adaptations of shows like *Jesus Christ Superstar* (1973) and *Hair* (1979) were also leaving the traditional audience behind.

> ### *Sounding off*
>
> *Despite the film's huge success, co-star Christopher Plummer was not a fan of* The Sound of Music *(1965). He once referred to it as 'The Sound of Mucus' and regretted turning down the role of secret agent Harry Palmer in* The Ipcress File *(1965) in order to play Captain von Trapp in the musical.*

Three British musicals

While Hollywood indisputably remained the home of the movie musical, three films emerged from the UK in the sixties and seventies that would – in their very different ways – take their place among the best. Significantly, all three films were made by directors fresh to the genre, which in part explains their distinctive styles.

Oliver! (1968), with words and music by Lionel Bart, was directed by Carol Reed who was best known for his black-and-white screen dramas of the forties. In *Oliver!* he successfully blended the stage show's exuberance with the brutal melodrama of Charles Dickens's novel, extracting memorable performances from Ron Moody as Fagin and Oliver Reed (the director's nephew) as Bill Sikes.

Oliver Reed also appears in *Tommy* (1975), a mystical rock opera directed by the *enfant terrible* of British film, Ken Russell. The story – a deaf, dumb and blind child is eventually cured and becomes a rock star – was written by Pete Townshend of The Who, with the group's lead singer Roger Daltrey in the title role. Excessive, surreal and loud, it showcases rock stars like Elton John and Eric Clapton and, for anyone seeking an antidote to *The Sound of Music*, is an exhilarating experience.

Bugsy Malone (1976) was director Alan Parker's first feature film. A musical gangster spoof with all the parts played by children, one of whom is the 13-year-old Jodie Foster, it has songs by the Oscar-nominated Paul Williams. *Bugsy* launched Parker on a long career in movies that would include a musical of an altogether different tempo – Andrew Lloyd Webber and Tim Rice's *Evita* (1996), with Madonna playing Argentina's First Lady.

Travolta fever

Saturday Night Fever (1977) introduced John Travolta, already a TV star, to the big screen. In Brooklyn, Saturday night is disco night – and 'King of the Disco' is Tony Manero, played (or rather danced) by John Travolta. Slickly directed by John Badham and featuring songs from the Bee Gees, the film was a colossal box-office success.

Within a year Travolta, now a major movie star, was back on the screen, this time in *Grease*, based on the stage musical and set in a fifties American high school. The lead role of Danny was originally offered to Henry Winkler (the Fonz in TV's *Happy Days*), but the actor declined to be typecast as another fifties teen character. Any shortfalls in the production were swiftly forgotten in the phenomenal response to the movie, which took the teenage market by storm and has led to *Grease* becoming the highest grossing musical to date in the USA.

In 1983 John Travolta returned as the disco king Tony Manero, in the sequel *Staying Alive*. The film was written and directed by Sylvester Stallone and once again had songs from the Bee Gees. Unlike *Saturday Night Fever*, the movie was panned by the critics but Travolta fans, staying alive and loyal, handed their hero another box-office hit.

Turning on the tap

For his role as the smooth-talking lawyer Billy Flynn in the musical Chicago *(2002), actor Richard Gere was not only required to sing but also to perform a solo tap-dance routine – something he had never done before. He refused to audition his singing voice but got the part anyway, and then had to undergo three months of intensive tap-dancing lessons before he was ready for the cameras. His rhythmical performance was a revelation to critics and fans alike.* Chicago *went on to collect six Oscars (though Gere wasn't among the recipients) and became the first musical to win 'Best Picture' since* Oliver! *in 1968.*

Les Mis

In 2012 the long-awaited *Les Misérables* arrived on the big screen, 27 years after its stage debut in London (and exactly 150 years after Victor Hugo's novel was first published). Tom Hooper, whose previous film *The King's Speech* had earned him an Oscar, directed the movie. In a brave departure from traditional film technique, the songs were sung live on the set instead of being pre-recorded. Since none of the performers were primarily singers this was a challenging exercise for all concerned.

There were other challenges too. At one stage of the production Hugh Jackman (playing Jean Valjean) was deprived of liquids for 36 hours in order to affect a suitably gaunt appearance. And co-star Anne Hathaway rapidly shed 11 kilos and sacrificed much of her hair to play the dying Fantine. It's not called *Les Misérables* for nothing.

Female dancing partners shared by Fred Astaire and Gene Kelly

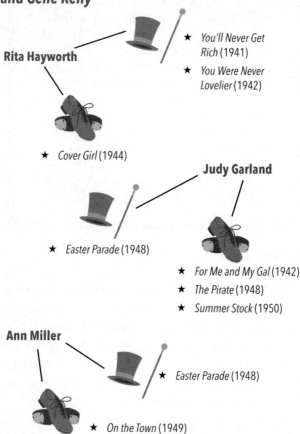

Rita Hayworth

★ *You'll Never Get Rich* (1941)
★ *You Were Never Lovelier* (1942)

★ *Cover Girl* (1944)

Judy Garland

★ *Easter Parade* (1948)

★ *For Me and My Gal* (1942)
★ *The Pirate* (1948)
★ *Summer Stock* (1950)

Ann Miller

★ *Easter Parade* (1948)

★ *On the Town* (1949)

Footnote: *Fred Astaire and Gene Kelly only worked together in one feature film. In the 1946 movie The Ziegfeld Follies, they performed a George Gershwin comedy song-and-dance number, 'The Babbit and the Bromide'.*

Vera-Ellen

★ *Three Little Words* (1950)
★ *The Belle of New York* (1952)

★ *Words and Music* (1948)
★ *On the Town* (1949)

Cyd Charisse

★ *The Band Wagon* (1953)
★ *Silk Stockings* (1957)

★ *Singin' in the Rain* (1952)
★ *Brigadoon* (1954)
★ *It's Always Fair Weather* (1955)

Leslie Caron

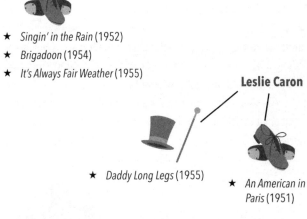

★ *Daddy Long Legs* (1955)

★ *An American in Paris* (1951)

Fred Astaire   Gene Kelly

CHAPTER 6

HOW THE WEST WAS WON

I made over forty Westerns. I used to lie awake nights trying to think up new ways of getting on and off a horse.

WILLIAM WYLER, DIRECTOR

The popular Wild West shows of frontiersmen like Colonel 'Buffalo Bill' Cody laid the groundwork for the Western movie. The early one-reel films were shot in the woods of New Jersey, where the first studios were based, and consisted of little more than a pursuit and a shoot-out. The first Western movie star was Gilbert M. Anderson, better known as 'Bronco Billy'. A former vaudeville performer (his real name was Max Aronson), he appeared in more than 350 short films, many of which he directed himself. In Edwin S. Porter's milestone movie *The Great Train Robbery* (1903), the prolific Anderson played no less than three parts in the film's 11 minutes.

Hollywood's pioneers were quick to take advantage of the dramatic scenery in California and its neighbouring states, much of which became the natural habitat of the Western. Monument Valley, on the border of Arizona and Utah, was the backdrop for countless films, not least those of director John Ford who described it as the 'most complete, beautiful and peaceful place on earth' – except presumably when it had 'cowboys and Indians' thundering through it. Wild West towns were erected on studio backlots, complete with sheriff's office, corral and saloon. For the next 50 years or so the Western was a cornerstone of American film-making. Hollywood's highly romanticised version of the frontier would bear little relation to the truth, but as a character says in Ford's film *The Man Who Shot Liberty Valance* (1962), 'When the legend becomes fact, print the legend.'

Hat code

In the early black-and-white days of the Western, cinema audiences could usually tell the good guy from the bad guy by the colour of his hat. Heroes sported a white Stetson, villains were topped off in black. The code was first introduced in Edwin S. Porter's The Great Train Robbery *(1903) and carried on well into the thirties. One man visibly bucked the trend. Hopalong Cassidy (played by William Boyd) always dressed from head to toe in black; but no one could mistake the squeaky-clean Hopalong for a bad guy.*

Silent in the saddle

The two greatest Western stars of the silent era were William S. Hart (the 'S' stood for Surrey) and Tom Mix, though their screen personas could hardly have been more different. Hart was born in New York but grew up in the frontier states of Minnesota and Wisconsin, learning to speak Sioux as a child. In his teens he worked as a ranch hand, developing skills in the saddle that he would later transfer with good effect to the silver screen. Despite this background, he became an established Broadway actor, often in Shakespearean roles, before gravitating to Hollywood. A friend of legendary lawmen Wyatt Earp and Bat Masterson, Hart injected a degree of gritty realism into his films. He often played outlaws, men with a rugged moral code of their own, and portrayed the seamier side of life in the West.

By the mid-twenties Hart's popularity was on the wane. The public had had their fill of his dour dramas and looked for a more stylish Western hero. The clean-cut, white-hatted Tom Mix fitted the bill. No one could doubt his credentials for the job. He had seen action in the 1898 Spanish–American War and in China's Boxer Rebellion of 1900, since when he had worked as a cowpuncher and rodeo rider. But his films were the antithesis of Hart's. Tom Mix was always the  good guy, managing to triumph over the baddies without getting his hands, or his hat, dirty. When the talkies came in, Mix rode off into the sunset of retirement, with a substantial fortune to keep him company.

John Ford

He once introduced himself at a meeting of fellow Hollywood directors with the words, 'My name is John Ford. I make Westerns.' In fact, Ford made a wide variety of films, but it is for his Westerns that he remains best known to movie audiences. His first major Western was *The Iron Horse*, a silent film made in 1924 about the building of the railroad. Fifteen years later came *Stagecoach* (1939), which made a star out of John Wayne (fortunately for him Gary Cooper had turned down the role of the Ringo Kid) and started a working relationship between actor and director that lasted for a quarter of a century. Wayne starred in all three of the so-called 'Cavalry Trilogy' – *Fort Apache* (1948), *She Wore a Yellow Ribbon* (1949) and *Rio Grande* (1950) – and in later films such as *The Searchers* (1956), *The Horse Soldiers* (1959) and *The Man Who Shot Liberty Vallance* (1962).

Ford liked working with his stock company of character actors, as well as with certain stars. Henry Fonda and James Stewart were two of the latter. Fonda played Wyatt Earp in Ford's *My Darling Clementine* (1946) and co-starred with John Wayne in *Fort Apache*. Stewart was in *Two Rode Together* (1961) and *Cheyenne Autumn* (1964), the director's final Western, as well as in *Liberty Vallance*. Shot amongst stunning scenery and full of engagingly spirited characters, Ford's movies express nostalgia for an Old West that never really existed but one that is always worth looking at.

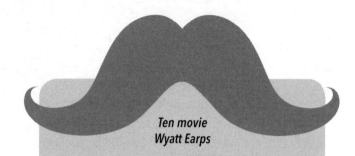

Ten movie
Wyatt Earps

Randolph Scott (Frontier Marshall, 1939)

Henry Fonda (My Darling Clementine, 1946)

Will Geer (Winchester '73, 1950)

Joel McCrea (Wichita, 1955)

Burt Lancaster (Gunfight at the O.K. Corral, 1957)

James Stewart (Cheyenne Autumn, 1964)

Guy Madison (Gunmen of the Rio Grande, 1964)

James Garner (Hour of the Gun, 1967)

Kurt Russell (Tombstone, 1993)

Kevin Costner (Wyatt Earp, 1994)

Western landmarks

The 20 years that followed the end of World War Two were the heyday of the Western. The singing cowboys Gene Autry and Roy Rogers were still in full throttle, mounted on their 'four-legged friends', Champion and Trigger respectively. Countless 'B' Westerns shared the bill with the main feature, and the Wild West became familiar territory on television.

Among the landmark movies of the period were: *Red River* (1946) and *Rio Bravo* (1958), both starring John Wayne and directed by Howard Hawks; Anthony Mann's *Winchester '73* (1950), one of five quality Westerns he made with James Stewart; George Stevens' *Shane* (1953) with a heroically neat Alan Ladd in the title role; Sam Peckinpah's *Ride the High Country* (1961) and *The Wild Bunch* (1969) – the latter's bloody climax, orchestrated by the machine gun, tipping the genre towards a more violent future.

High Noon

High Noon (1952) was made by Fred Zinnemann, a director not normally associated with Westerns. The film starred Gary Cooper as a town marshal fighting a lone battle against the odds. Carl Foreman, who wrote the screenplay, was a victim of the anti-Communist witch-hunts taking place in Hollywood at the time and the movie has been seen as a political allegory. Blacklisted by the studios, Foreman moved to the UK and wrote *The Bridge on the River Kwai* (1957) and *The Guns of Navarone* (1961) among others.

Playing her first major screen role was Grace Kelly, who primly turned up for her audition wearing white gloves, like the young society woman she was. Rivalling her for Cooper's affections in the film is the sultry Mexican actress Katy Jurado, who resented the fact that Zinnemann favoured the blonde Kelly when it came to close-ups. The 50-year-old Cooper was suffering from arthritis and recovering from a hernia operation, but still managed to hold his own in a vigorous fist fight with deputy Lloyd Bridges (father of Jeff) and without the aid of a stunt double. Shot in just 32 days, *High Noon* deserved its four Oscars, which included one for the stoical 'Coop'.

Not so magnificent

One of the most successful Westerns ever, *The Magnificent Seven* (1960) spawned three sequels, all grossly inferior to the magnificent original. The director John Sturges already had some fine Westerns under his belt, including *Gunfight at the O.K. Corral* (1957), and a strong cast and Elmer Bernstein's stirring theme music added to the mix.

However, the on-screen camaraderie between the two main characters, Chris (Yul Brynner) and Vin (Steve McQueen), was not reflected off-camera. There was an unpleasant rivalry between the two actors, McQueen resenting Brynner's star status and his sizeable entourage of minders. Having grown up on a farm in the mid-West, McQueen was adept with horses and guns and would upstage the less competent, Russian-born Brynner at every opportunity. The feud got into the papers and Sturges had his hands full keeping the peace. Happily none of this is apparent as we watch them ride side by side, loyal comrades in arms – but then that's what acting is all about.

Spaghetti Westerns

The first major Italian-style Western was the 1964 movie *A Fistful of Dollars*, directed by Sergio Leone and starring Clint Eastwood. The film was typical of the 'Spaghetti' genre in that it had an Italian director and crew, a cast made up of several nationalities and was shot in Spain. Since the cast of these hybrid Westerns was usually multilingual, dialogue was kept to a minimum (action being seen to speak louder than words) and post-synchronised in Italian for a domestic audience. By American standards the movies were cheap to make, with the budget sometimes able to stretch to a fading Hollywood star or, in the case of *A Fistful of Dollars*, one on the rise. Unlike in the traditional Western movie, the moral distinction between good and evil is not always clear. The Clint Eastwood character, for example, is no less reluctant to kill than those he comes up against.

The Italian Western, elevated in status by Sergio Leone, lasted from the early sixties to the late seventies, though it wasn't the first on the European scene. In 1961 Michael Carreras (later head of Hammer Films) directed *The Savage Guns*, an Anglo–Spanish production starring Hollywood actor Richard Basehart as a gunslinger. As for the term 'Spaghetti Western', it was a phrase dismissively coined by an Italian film critic. Hopefully, he was later made to eat his words.

Dollars saga

Clint Eastwood, fresh from the TV series *Rawhide*, had not been Sergio Leone's initial choice for the lead role in *A Fistful of Dollars*. Henry Fonda, Charles Bronson, James Coburn, Rory Calhoun, Steve Reeves and Ty Hardin had all been considered ahead of him.

For the second film of what would become known as the 'Dollars Trilogy' – *For a Few Dollars More* (1965) – Eastwood was joined by Lee Van Cleef as Colonel Mortimer. Like his co-star, Van Cleef had not been the director's first pick. Lee Marvin had originally accepted the part but dumped it for the dual role in the comedy Western *Cat Ballou* (1965), for which he won an Oscar. A year later came *The Good, the Bad and the Ugly* – played by Clint Eastwood, Lee Van Cleef and Eli Wallach respectively. It was the last time Leone and Eastwood worked together. The relationship between them had been a difficult one, not least because of the language problem, and when Leone offered the actor the lead role of 'Harmonica' in his next film, *Once Upon a Time in the West*, Eastwood declined.

The international success of these films had brought Sergio Leone quite a few dollars more. The budget for *Once Upon a Time in the West* (1968) was large enough to recruit three major Hollywood stars – Henry Fonda (for once playing a villain), Charles Bronson and Jason Robards – as well as Italy's Claudia Cardinale. A sprawling epic on a much grander scale than the earlier movies, it is unquestionably the Italian director's finest Western.

There is a touching footnote to Sergio Leone's life in the movies. The director died in 1989 of heart failure, aged 60. At the time of his death he was watching a film on television, at his home in Rome – its title: *I Want to Live!*

Name changers

To disguise the 'Spaghetti' provenance of A Fistful of Dollars (1964), several of the Italian cast and crew adopted American-sounding names for the credits of the US-released version. Director Sergio Leone became 'Bob Robertson' (in homage to his film-director father Vincenzo Leone, whose professional name was Roberto Roberti). Actor Gian Maria Volonté changed his name to 'Johnny Wells'. Art director Carlo Simi opted for 'Charles Simons' and composer Ennio Morricone morphed into 'Leo Nichols'. They needn't have worried. Despite its pedigree (or indeed because of it) the film triumphed at the box office.

Clint Eastwood

By the seventies the Western was dying on its feet. Many of the great directors had left the scene and younger movie audiences were more attracted to science fiction and horror, or to urban-based dramas. There was a political sensitivity about the portrayal of Native Americans in particular and in any case the public had had a surfeit of Westerns on television.

Like a character in one of his films, the lone figure of Clint Eastwood rode to the rescue, reviving interest in the genre. *High Plains Drifter* (1972) and *Pale Rider* (1985) owe much to the 'Spaghetti' Western, with Eastwood once again playing the monosyllabic stranger. *The Outlaw Josey Wales* (1976) is a much more interesting film, the inevitable Eastwood violence tempered by humour and an assortment of attractively odd characters.

In 1992 came *Unforgiven*, a harsh, brutal vision of the Old West with Clint Eastwood as an ex-gunslinger called to action one last time. Gene Hackman (who collected an Oscar for his performance in the film) and Eastwood 'regular' Morgan Freeman are both outstanding, and Richard Harris contributes a memorable cameo. Eastwood missed out as Best Actor, but had the consolation of walking away with Oscars for Best Director and Best Picture. The Western was back in town.

Striking a chord

Music is an essential component of a Western, whether it be the quickening tempo of the chase, the menacing rhythm of Apache drums or the lush strains that accompany the unfolding landscape. Any list of the greatest Western themes (quite rightly a personal choice) would probably include Elmer Bernstein's spirited contribution to *The Magnificent Seven* (1960), Jerome Moross's expansive overture to *The Big Country* (1958), John Barry's moody melody from *Dances with Wolves* (1990) and Dimitri Tiomkin's title song for *High Noon* (1952) – sung on the soundtrack by Tex Ritter but a global hit for Frankie Laine.

In recent times, however, one composer has stood out from all the others: Ennio Morricone, whose distinctive music has played an even more integral role in the films of Sergio Leone and other directors in the genre. Morricone and Leone were at school together in the third grade but didn't get together professionally for another 25 years, until the director hired his former schoolmate to write the music for *A Fistful of Dollars* – and then for all his movies thereafter. Morricone's memorable compositions involving chimes, whistles, cracking whips, the Jew's harp and the human voice (with the composer's own speciality, the trumpet, often to the fore), are perfectly attuned to the casual violence and dark humour in Leone's films. The astonishingly prolific Morricone has composed over 500 scores for cinema and television, though only around 30 of these have been for Westerns – enough to have left his mark.

Last round-up

There are still plenty of Westerns being made, though significantly the genre rarely commands the attention of top directors as much as it used to do. Two of the best films in recent times have been remakes. The film *3.10 to Yuma* (2007), starring Russell Crowe and Christian Bale, came out 50 years after its predecessor. The original Delmer Daves' black-and-white film of the same name, with Glenn Ford and Van Heflin in the leading roles, was 30 minutes shorter and predictably less violent (though no less tense). The jury is still out as to which film takes the honours.

In 2010 Joel and Ethan Coen presented their version of *True Grit*, with Jeff Bridges playing the hard-drinking, one-eyed US marshal Rooster Cogburn. Forty years before, John Wayne had received his solitary Oscar for the same role in Henry Hathaway's 1969 film. Observant viewers spotted that in the intervening period Rooster's eye patch had moved from his left eye to his right. The Coen brothers' movie is much closer in tone to the Charles Portis novel on which both films are based, and there are impressive acting performances from Bridges and newcomer Hailee Steinfeld as Mattie Ross (Kim Darby in the original). The film received ten Oscar nominations but rode away empty-handed.

Major international film festivals

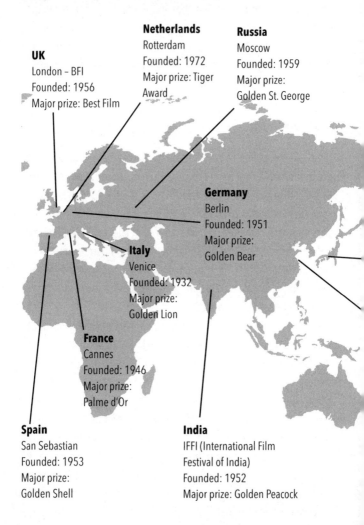

UK
London – BFI
Founded: 1956
Major prize: Best Film

Netherlands
Rotterdam
Founded: 1972
Major prize: Tiger Award

Russia
Moscow
Founded: 1959
Major prize:
Golden St. George

Germany
Berlin
Founded: 1951
Major prize:
Golden Bear

Italy
Venice
Founded: 1932
Major prize:
Golden Lion

France
Cannes
Founded: 1946
Major prize:
Palme d'Or

Spain
San Sebastian
Founded: 1953
Major prize:
Golden Shell

India
IFFI (International Film
Festival of India)
Founded: 1952
Major prize: Golden Peacock

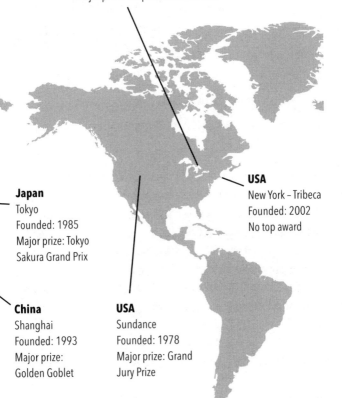

Canada
Toronto
Founded: 1976
Major prize: People's Choice Award

USA
New York – Tribeca
Founded: 2002
No top award

Japan
Tokyo
Founded: 1985
Major prize: Tokyo
Sakura Grand Prix

China
Shanghai
Founded: 1993
Major prize:
Golden Goblet

USA
Sundance
Founded: 1978
Major prize: Grand
Jury Prize

CHAPTER 7

CLOSE ENCOUNTERS OF ALL KINDS

The monster was the best friend I ever had.
BORIS KARLOFF, ACTOR

In 1902, the French magician and pioneer film-maker Georges Méliès sent a cannon-propelled rocket to the moon. The moon had a human face, pockmarked with craters, and the rocket landed smack in its right eye. Méliès' film *Le voyage dans la lune* (*The Trip to the Moon*) crams 30 imaginative tableaux into its 13 minutes, mixing pantomime violence with moments of humour. The moon is inhabited by creatures called Selenites, who live in a sub-lunar forest of giant mushrooms. The visiting scientists (whose leader is played by Méliès himself) capture one of the Selenites and bring it safely back to Earth, where they receive an ecstatic welcome. Audiences were thrilled by the director's cinematic sleight of hand, with special effects never seen before. His success was not destined to last, though his legacy has. Following a series of financial setbacks, the ingenious Méliès was declared bankrupt and ended his days running a confectionery stall at a Parisian railway station.

Future shocks

Twenty-five years later, in Germany, Fritz Lang gave cinemagoers a different glimpse of the future with his film *Metropolis* (1927). Set in the year 2000, the two-and-a-half-hour-long silent movie takes place in a gigantic urban dystopia called Metropolis. Most of the set was created in miniature form, the live action skilfully combined with models and painted backdrops through the use of specially designed and positioned mirrors that had the effect of reducing the actors in proportion to the background. It was a technique that would be used again and again. Lang's groundbreaking film also included the soon-to-be-familiar duo of a mad scientist and his robot.

In the years since then, science fiction has taken on many different forms: journeys into and out of space, wars between worlds and all sorts of aliens. Less frivolous have been the post-apocalyptic wastelands and potential collisions with asteroids and the like. Sci-fi and horror often overlap, with monsters bursting out of the sea, mutations bursting out of laboratories and aliens bursting out of swollen stomachs, not to mention a cinema audience that is always bursting for more.

Frankenstein's monster

Nineteen thirty-one gave birth to two seminal horror films – *Frankenstein* and *Dracula*. Cast as the monster in the first of these was Boris Karloff (real name William Henry Pratt), a cricket-loving Englishman who had been playing bit parts in Hollywood movies for some 12 years. He had not been the original choice. Lon Chaney, the 'Man of a Thousand Faces', had been earmarked to play both Frankenstein's creation and Dracula (Universal Studios made both films) but had died of cancer before he could get started. The next in line, Hungarian actor Béla Lugosi, accepted the part of Dracula, which he had been playing on stage, but declined the non-speaking role of the monster. *Frankenstein*'s English director James Whale had spotted Karloff in the studio canteen, a tall man with a gaunt, lugubrious face and a lumbering walk.

Much of the credit for the success of the monster (and the film) must go to the make-up artist Jack Pierce, who redefined Karloff's features with layers of cheesecloth and stiffened his gait with boots that weighed 8 kg (18 lb) apiece. Mortician's wax was applied to his eyelids to give a half-closed effect, and wire clamps pulled down the corners of his mouth. The touchingly bewildered sensitivity of the monster was down to Boris Karloff himself. By the time he reappeared in *The Bride of Frankenstein* 4 years later, the actor was famous enough to be billed simply as 'Karloff'.

Specialists in horror

One man who did play both Frankenstein's monster and the vampire Count was Christopher Lee, who made his name in a series of productions for the British company Hammer Films. Unlike the slightly built Béla Lugosi, the London-born Lee was tall, dark and handsome with a deep, powerful voice, his saturnine features courtesy of his Italian mother. Altogether he appeared as Count Dracula eight times, starting with *Dracula* in 1958. In *The Curse of Frankenstein* (1957) he began an on-screen partnership with Peter Cushing, who played opposite him as Baron Frankenstein and in later films as the vampire hunter Van Helsing.

The sinisterly sibilant Vincent Price, an established movie actor if not quite a star, made his 'horror' debut in *The House of Wax* in 1953, the first 3D movie to have stereophonic sound. Thereafter he appeared in a series of low-budget movies adapted from Edgar Allan Poe stories – *The House of Usher* (1960), *The Pit and the Pendulum* (1961), *The Raven* (1962) and *The Masque of the Red Death* (1964) among them. The films catapulted Price to stardom and made him the undisputed king of horror, though a teasing sense of humour always seemed to lurk beneath the menace.

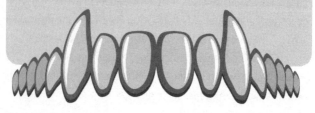

Ten great blood-sucking movies to get your teeth into

Film	Director
Nosferatu (1922)	F. W. Murnau
Dracula (1931)	Tod Browning
Horror of Dracula (1958)	Terence Fisher
Fright Night (1985)	Tom Holland
Near Dark (1987)	Kathryn Bigelow
Cronos (1993)	Guillermo del Toro
Interview with the Vampire (1994)	Neil Jordan
From Dusk Till Dawn (1996)	Robert Rodriguez
Let the Right One In (2008)	Tomas Alfredson
Twilight (2008)	Catherine Hardwicke

Space odyssey

The sixties space race between the US and the Soviet Union brought a more thoughtful and at times more informed approach to sci-fi movies. Scientific mishaps still upchucked monstrous creatures from the deep and misshapen aliens continued to invade planet Earth. However, the possibilities of space exploration, and what it might lead to, began to be taken more seriously. It was against this background that the American film-maker Stanley Kubrick, domiciled in the UK, made what many believe to be the greatest science-fiction film to date.

2001: A Space Odyssey was released in 1968. Based on a short story by Arthur C. Clarke called 'The Sentinel', the film is about the mysterious forces (manifested in the form of a black monolith) that control human evolution, beginning in prehistoric times and ending with a mission to Jupiter. Shot entirely in England, the film's state-of-the-art special effects give rise to some visually stunning sequences: an animal bone hurled into the air by a man-ape becomes a slowly revolving spaceship; spacecraft melodically float through infinite expanses of space to the lush strains of the 'Blue Danube Waltz'; the demise of the mutinous onboard computer HAL is conveyed by its discordant efforts to sing the music-hall song 'Daisy, Daisy...'. And why '2001'? Well, in 1968 it seemed a millennium away, though some believe it was in homage to Fritz Lang's *Metropolis*, set a futuristic year earlier.

Shock treatments

Roman Polanski's 1968 movie *Rosemary's Baby* – about devil worship in affluent Manhattan – signalled a move away from traditional Gothic horror and three seventies shockers followed the trend. *The Exorcist* (1973), adapted by William Peter Blatty from his own novel, is about a girl possessed by demonic forces (a decade earlier, and doubtless in a sunnier mood, Blatty had written the Pink Panther movie *A Shot in the Dark*). *The Omen*, another diabolical tale, and Stephen King's story *Carrie* both hit the screen in 1976. A new generation of film-makers had taken over the genre and brought it shockingly up to date. Horror had moved from Transylvania to Pennsylvania and was lurking in a suburb near you.

John Carpenter's *Halloween* (1978) launched a horror franchise that 30 years later had moved into double figures, though Carpenter himself only directed the original (made for $300,000, it grossed over $12 million). His next outing in horror territory was *The Fog* (1980) in which a lethal Californian pea-souper is populated by leprous ghosts. Wes Craven's *A Nightmare on Elm Street* (1984) was another scary blockbuster that created an extended franchise. Raised a Baptist, Craven was college age before he saw his first movie and began his professional life as a university professor, since when he has left a gruesome trail of flesh-creepers behind him.

Two directors faithfully returned to the source material, underlining the fact by building the author's name into the film's title. Francis Ford Coppola's 1992 movie *Bram Stoker's Dracula* is a visually puffed-up version of the story with Gary Oldman in the title role. Two years later came *Mary Shelley's Frankenstein*, directed by and starring Kenneth Branagh as the obsessed scientist, with Robert De Niro as his monstrous creation. But good intentions are seldom enough, and neither film matches its 1931 predecessor.

Movie howler

In Harry Potter and the Order of the Phoenix *(2007), a sleeping Harry can be seen wearing a light-blue striped T-shirt. But when a vision of Voldemort prompts him suddenly to sit up in bed, his shirt has changed into a solid dark blue number with buttons. Now that is magic.*

Very special effects

Modern special effects, and in particular computer-generated imagery (CGI), have enabled science-fiction film-makers (and others) to spread their wings. Michael Crichton's *Westworld* (1973), about a robotic gunslinger (Yul Brynner) that goes berserk in a Western theme park, was the first feature film to employ CGI. Now no self-respecting sci-fi movie would be seen without it.

There is no doubting the CGI credentials of *The Matrix* (1999), a virtual-reality blockbuster written and directed by the Wachowski duo, Andy and Lana, and shot in Australia. The film owes a debt to video games and to kung-fu movies, though the fast-paced narrative (sometimes at the expense of continuity) is all its own. Artificial intelligence, philosophy and the 'we shall overcome' spirit of the human race are combined with technical wizardry to create an eye-popping experience. The film gave rise to two sequels, *The Matrix Reloaded* and *The Matrix Revolutions* (both released in 2003), though the final part of the trilogy falls some way short of the original. *The Matrix*, with its super slo-mo 'bullet time' and other special effects, has left its impression on many movies since, from *Wanted* (2008) to *Inception* (2010).

Star flaws

In the meantime, the Force continues to be with *Star Wars* and its 'expanded universe' – as its multimedia spread of TV series, video games, books and comics is called. The first three films, which came out at three-yearly intervals (1977–1983), were followed by a prequel trilogy (1999–2005) with the same release pattern. A further trilogy is in production.

Star Wars has created its own intergalactic lexicon and a galaxy of special effects and technical gizmos. Not that everything has always worked smoothly. Crammed inside the robot R2-D2 was the 3ft 8in (112 cm) tall Kenny Baker. When shooting the desert sequences for the original film, in Tunisia in 1976, the robot's controls packed up and R2-D2 had to be pulled along by a nylon rope. When finally the machine did work it made such a clatter that the only way to let Baker know that the shot was in the can was to bang on the exterior with a hammer.

The voice of E.T.

The distinctive sounds emanating from the eponymous extra-terrestrial of Steven Spielberg's film did not come easily. E.T.'s 'voice' was the creation of the Academy Award-winning sound-effects designer Ben Burtt who used an amalgam of animal noises and human voices to achieve the desired effect. The principal contributor was an elderly actress named Pat Welsh whose daily inhalation of 40 cigarettes had given her voice the required croaky quality. Others recorded by Burtt included Spielberg himself and the sound man's own sleeping wife, who had a cold at the time and whose blocked nasal passages provided a valuable 'snuffling' element. The plaintive 'E.T., phone home', one of the film's most memorable lines, was delivered by the actress Debra Winger.

Topping the terminator

The Canadian-born James Cameron began his movie career in the art department building miniature sets – a modest enough start for a man who went on to create the two highest grossing movies of all time (*Avatar* and *Titanic*). His breakthrough film as a director was *The Terminator* (1984), with Arnold Schwarzenegger perfectly cast as something other than human. The movie was a great success and Cameron followed it two years later with *Aliens*, a sequel to Ridley Scott's 1971 sci-fi horror film. Cameron's innovative special effects got a further outing in *Terminator 2: Judgement Day* (1991) after which the director's attention was diverted from science fiction by things *Titanic* (1997).

Cameron's next feature film, *Avatar* (2009) had been under development for over ten years, the director holding off for a while to allow technology to catch up with his concept. The movie spectacularly combines live action with computer-generated animation, with many of the visual effects created in New Zealand by Weta Digital – a company co-founded by fellow director Peter Jackson. At one stage more than 900 people were employed on the project.

A 3D version of the movie was released, enhancing the extraordinary effects and boosting the reputation of three-dimensional film, which has had a somewhat chequered career since its introduction in the 1950s. *Avatar* became the first film to earn $2 billion worldwide, at the same time spreading its core message about protecting the environment. That's if you can spot it with everything else going on.

Sci-fi theme chart

War zone
The War of the Worlds (1953)
Star Wars series (1977–)
Battlestar Galactica (1978)
Starship Troopers (1997)
War of the Worlds (2005)

Time travel
The Time Machine (1960)
Planet of the Apes (1968)
The Final Countdown (1980)
Back to the Future (1985)
Primer (2004)

Out in space
Le voyage dans la lune (1902)
Forbidden Planet (1956)
2001: A Space Odyssey (1968)
Solaris (1972)
Sunshine (2007)
Moon (2009)
Galaxy (2013)
Interstellar (2014)

Aliens
The Day the Earth Stood Still (1951)
It Came from Outer Space (1953)
Close Encounters of the Third Kind (1977)
Alien (1979)
The Thing (1982)
E.T. the Extra-Terrestrial (1982)
Aliens (1986)
District 9 (2009)

Unnatural phenomena

Godzilla (1954)
The Quatermass Experiment (1955)
The Fly (1986)
Jurassic Park (1993)
Cloverfield (2008)
Monsters (2010)

Eco disasters

Silent Running (1971)
Soylent Green (1973)
Mad Max (1979)
Children of Men (2006)
Avatar (2009)

Androids and robots

Westworld (1973)
Blade Runner (1982)
The Terminator (1984)
Robocop (1987)
*Terminator 2:
Judgement Day* (1991)
Transformers series (2007–)

Utopias and dystopias

Metropolis (1927)
Things to Come (1936)
A Clockwork Orange (1971)
Logan's Run (1976)
The Matrix (1999)
Minority Report (2002)
The Hunger Games (2012)

CHAPTER 8

GETTING ANIMATED

*I only hope that we don't lose sight of one thing
– that it was all started by a mouse.*

WALT DISNEY, ANIMATOR AND FILM-MAKER

Until the advent of computer graphics at the back end of the twentieth century, most animated films started as hand-drawn illustrations. An early exponent of the technique was the French animator Emile Cohl, a former political cartoonist who embarked on a film career at the age of 50. The story goes that Cohl was offered a job by Gaumont Studios in Paris after he had accused them of plagiarising one of his cartoons for a movie poster. Cohl (real name Emile Courtet) created an amiable *petit homme* called Fantoche who featured in several animated films, the best known of which is *Phantasmagoria* (1908).

The oldest surviving animated feature film is *The Adventures of Prince Achmed* (*Die Abenteuer des Prinzen Achmed*), based on a tale from the *Arabian Nights* and produced in Germany in 1926. By this time animated cartoons were becoming increasingly popular, especially in the USA. The Fleischer Studios, located in New York, created enduring characters like the Jazz Age flapper Betty Boop and Popeye the Sailor. MGM set Tom and Jerry on their unending collision course and Warner Bros. launched *Merrie Melodies* and *Looney Tunes*, populated by the likes of Bugs Bunny, Sylvester the Cat, Tweety Bird and the Road Runner.

World of Disney

Walt Disney claimed that Mickey Mouse 'popped out of my mind onto a drawing pad' during a train journey from New York to Hollywood, at a time when the animation company he had set up with his brother Roy was about to hit the rails. It changed their fortunes. The public had its first glimpse of Mickey in *Steamboat Willie* (1928), an eight-minute talkie released ahead of two silent cartoons featuring the mouse and made the same year. It was love at first sight, and soon Mickey had replaced Felix the Cat as the world's number one cartoon character.

Before long, Mickey and his girlfriend Minnie (short for Minerva) were joined by Donald Duck, Goofy and Pluto, all of whom 'starred' in their own cartoons. In 1929, Disney launched a series of musical shorts called *Silly Symphonies*, one of which, *Flowers and Trees* (1932), became the first cartoon to win an Oscar. A year later came *The Three Little Pigs* with its hit song 'Who's Afraid of the Big Bad Wolf', probably the most viewed cartoon of all time. Some saw the film as a metaphor for the Great Depression (the 'Big Bad Wolf') with the song a rallying cry for the hardest hit.

Disney's folly

Despite the popular success of his *Silly Symphonies* and other shorts, Walt Disney knew that he had to move on to bigger and better things to make any headway in the industry. Animation was costly to produce and cartoon curtain-raisers didn't command the cinema rentals that feature films attracted. Yet many predicted that Disney's decision to make a feature-length animated movie, especially one aimed at children, would prove his downfall. They called it 'Disney's folly' – he called it *Snow White and the Seven Dwarfs*.

The 1937 film took more than three years to make and cost around $1.5 million, an enormous sum in those days. Some two million sketches and paintings were created, though less than ten per cent finally made it into the 83-minute film. Around 750 people were employed on the movie. One of them, the dancer Marge Belcher (better known as Marge Champion after her marriage to fellow dancer Gower Champion) was the human template, or movement model, for Snow White. To listen to the voice auditions for Snow White and the other characters, Disney had a speaker set up in his office, away from the sound stage, so that he wouldn't be influenced by what an actor looked like. The leading role went to a 19-year-old trainee opera singer, Adriana Caselotti.

The film was a box-office sensation, with Disney able to pay off all the money he had borrowed within six months. Two of the songs – 'Whistle While You Work' and 'Heigh Ho! It's Off To Work We Go' – became global hits. Two years after the film's release, its vindicated creator was given an honorary Oscar – along with seven miniature replicas.

Name-dropping

The names eventually bestowed on the Seven Dwarfs – Bashful, Doc, Dopey, Grumpy, Happy, Sleepy and Sneezy – didn't come easily. Among the 40 or so alternatives seriously mooted by the Disney screenwriters were: Baldy, Blabby, Deafy, Dirty, Gabby, Hoppy, Neurtsy, Shifty, Shorty, Sniffy, Soulful, Weepy and Wheezy. There was also Biggy-Wiggy, Biggo-Ego and Awful – which just about sums them up.

Toy stories

Had Pixar been more successful at selling computers, their core product, they might never have become a leading creative force in computer-generated film animation. As it was, their CGI promos for the product attracted more attention than the hardware itself and with funding from Steve Jobs, the founder of Apple, the company changed direction. A three-picture deal with Disney Studios followed, the first off the production line being the phenomenally successful *Toy Story* in 1995. It was cinema's first all-computer-animated feature film.

Since then Pixar, bought by Disney lock, stock and CGI in 2006, has produced a series of box-office blockbusters, among them *A Bug's Life* (1998), *Finding Nemo* (2003), *The Incredibles* (2004), *Ratatouille* (2007) and *Monsters University* (2013). Sandwiched between these have been two *Toy Story* sequels and a couple of *Cars*. Key to Pixar's success has been their ability to create stories that stretch children's minds as well as their imagination and at the same time have something in them for adults. *Wall-E* (2008) depicts a post-apocalyptic world, while *Up* (2009) entertainingly confronts old age – bridging the generation gap in more ways than one.

Right accent

With animated movies now part of cinema's mainstream, stars are queuing up to give voice to them. Tom Hanks has had three outings as Sheriff Woody in the *Toy Story* films. The stellar line-up for *Fantastic Mr Fox* (2009) includes George Clooney, Meryl Streep and Bill Murray, and *The Croods* (2013) are characterised by the far from prehistoric Nicholas Cage and Emma Stone, among others.

The first of the four *Shrek* films to date was released in 2001. Actor and comedian Chris Farley was signed up as the voice of the eponymous ogre and had almost completed recording the project when he died of a drug overdose at the age of 33. Mike Myers stepped into Farley's (and Shrek's) shoes, but insisted on having the script substantially rewritten to eliminate his predecessor's imprint. After the revised version had been fully recorded, Myers requested that he be allowed to do it all over again, but this time in a Scottish accent. As he later said in an interview, 'Because fairytales are a European thing and ogres are more earthy the Scottish accent just felt right.' Just as well he was able to do one, then.

Playing with plasticine

Less dominant in the marketplace than Pixar but in its own way no less impressive has been the Bristol-based studio Aardman, which specialises in stop-motion animation using clay or plasticine models. Founded in 1972, the company cut its teeth (if you can do that with plasticine) on its shape-changing character Morph, who featured in artist Tony Hart's television series for children. As the company modestly expanded, new animators were recruited. Among them was Nick Parks, whose five-minute film *Creature Comforts* (1989) innovatively and inexpensively used non-actors for the animal characters' voices and earned Aardman its first Academy Award.

The plasticine duo Wallace and Gromit made their screen debut in *A Grand Day Out* (1989), pipped at the Oscars post by *Creature Comforts*. Parks more than made up for it with his next three Wallace and Gromit productions – *The Wrong Trousers* (1993), *A Close Shave* (1995) and the feature-length *The Curse of the Were-Rabbit* (2005) – all of which collected the sought-after statuette. *Chicken Run* (2000) was another worldwide success for Aardman, but *Flushed Away* (2006), despite a vocal cast that includes Hugh Jackman, Kate Winslet and Ian McKellen, performed less well and abruptly brought to an end the company's partnership with the US production giant DreamWorks. However, Aardman seems to have barely missed a beat, adding *Arthur Christmas* (2011) and *Shaun the Sheep* (2015) to its malleable line-up of characters. The 'morph' the merrier, you might say!

Time and motion

The stop-motion technique requires patience as well as skill and inspiration. To achieve the effect of lifelike movement, the model is minutely adjusted between individually photographed frames. For Wallace's faithful canine companion Gromit to wag his tail for just ten seconds requires 120 separate shots. A few moments of screen time can take several days to shoot. And they say actors are tricky!

Oscar-winning songs from Disney animation films

1940	'When You Wish Upon a Star'	*Pinocchio*
1947	'Zip-a-Dee-Doo-Dah'	*Son of the South*
1989	'Under the Sea'	*The Little Mermaid*
1991	'Beauty and the Beast'	*Beauty and the Beast*
1992	'A Whole New World'	*Aladdin*
1994	'Can You Feel the Love Tonight?'	*The Lion King*
1995	'Colors of the Wind'	*Pocahontas*
1999	'You'll Be in My Heart'	*Tarzan*
2001	'If I Didn't Have You'	*Monsters, Inc*
2010	'We Belong Together'	*Toy Story 3*
2013	'Let It Go'	*Frozen*

The ten most expensive movies ever made

Film	Production costs (inflation adjusted)
Pirates of the Caribbean: At World's End (2007)	$341.8 million
Cleopatra (1963)	$339.5 million
Titanic (1997)	$294.3 million
Spider-Man 3 (2007)	$293.9 million
Tangled (2010)	$281.7 million
Harry Potter and the Half-Blood Prince (2009)	$275.3 million
Waterworld (1995)	$271.3 million
Pirates of the Caribbean: Dead Man's Chest (2006)	$263.7 million
Avatar (2009)	$261.0 million
The Hobbit (2012)	$257.2 million

CHAPTER 9

AND THE OSCAR GOES TO...

I'm just a girl from a trailer park who had a dream.
HILARY SWANK (ACCEPTING THE BEST ACTRESS AWARD IN 2004)

Former MGM boss Louis B. Mayer is the man we have to thank for the Oscars. It was Mayer's idea to set up the Academy of Motion Picture Arts and Sciences, an organisation that could mediate in labour disputes and help improve the image of the film industry whose reputation had been tarnished by a recent spate of scandals. The Academy was officially founded in 1927, with one of its stated objectives to award merit prizes on an annual basis.

The first Academy Awards ceremony took place in the Blossom Room of the Hollywood Roosevelt Hotel on 16 May 1929. By today's standards it was a modest affair, a sit-down dinner attended by 270 people. The Best Actor award went to the German star Emil Jannings and Janet Gaynor picked up the prize for Best Actress. The original award cited the actor's work in more than one film (in Jannings' case there were two, in Gaynor's three). However, within a couple of years the system was changed to the current practice of nominating an actor for a specific performance in a single film.

The Oscar

MGM's art director Cedric Gibbons came up with the initial design for the statuette – a knight standing on a reel of film – with Los Angeles sculptor George Stanley fashioning the model itself. The finished article stands 13.5 inches (34.29 cm) high and weighs 8.5 lb (3.6 kg). The gold is only skin deep, the bulk of the statuette being an amalgam of tin and copper. The five spokes on the reel represent the original branches of the Academy: actors, directors, producers, technicians and writers.

No one knows for sure how Oscar got its name. One popular theory credits the Academy's first librarian Margaret Herrick, who in 1931 is said to have observed that the statuette resembled her Uncle Oscar. Eight years later the Academy of Motion Picture Arts and Sciences officially dubbed the awards 'The Oscars'.

Ten Oscar 'firsts'

★ *First colour film to win Best Picture:* Gone with the Wind *(1939), directed by Victor Fleming.*

★ *First actor to receive a posthumous award: Peter Finch, Best Actor (*Network, *1976).*

★ *First actor to win an Oscar for playing a member of the opposite sex: Linda Hunt (*The Year of Living Dangerously, *1982).*

★ *First non-Hollywood film to win Best Picture:* Hamlet *(1948), starring and directed by Laurence Olivier.*

★ *First black actor to win an Oscar: Hattie McDaniel, Best Supporting Actress (*Gone with the Wind, *1939).*

★ *First black film-maker to win Best Picture: Steve McQueen (*12 Years a Slave, *2013).*

★ *First family to win Oscars across three generations: Walter Huston, Best Supporting Actor (*The Treasure of the Sierra Madre, *1948); son John Huston, Best Screenplay/Best Director for the same film; granddaughter Angelica Huston, Best Supporting Actress (*Prizzi's Honour, *1985) – directed by her father John Huston.*

★ *First British actor to win an Oscar on screen debut: Julie Andrews, Best Actress (*Mary Poppins, *1964).*

★ *First X-rated film to win Best Picture:* Midnight Cowboy *(1969), directed by John Schlesinger.*

★ *First actors to win separate Oscars for playing the same character: Marlon Brando (*The Godfather, *1972) and Robert De Niro (*The Godfather: Part II, *1974) as Vito Corleone.*

The British are coming

When, in 1982, Colin Welland won the award for Best Original Screenplay for *Chariots of Fire*, he excitedly warned the audience that 'the British are coming'. In truth, the British had arrived a long time before.

George Arliss was the first Brit to win an Academy Award, having been voted Best Actor for his performance in the title role of the 1929 film *Disraeli*. Arliss (billed on posters for the film as 'Mr George Arliss' to elevate him above his peers) was reprising a part he had played eight years before in a silent movie about the Victorian prime minister, which somewhat confusingly has the same title. Three years later Charles Laughton picked up the statuette for another historical portrayal, though one that was less reverential in tone – *The Private Life of Henry VIII* (1933).

Vivien Leigh's performance as Scarlet O'Hara in *Gone With the Wind* (1939) led her to become the first British recipient of the Best Actress award. (In 1952 she won it for a second time for *A Streetcar Named Desire*.) Joan Fontaine followed her in 1942, recognised for her role in Alfred Hitchcock's *Suspicion*, and a year later the award went to yet another British actress, Greer Garson, for the wartime tear-jerker *Mrs. Miniver*.

In 1930, Scottish-born Frank Lloyd became the first British director to win an Academy Award. Now largely forgotten, Lloyd won the Oscar for *The Divine Lady* (the story of Lady Hamilton's affair with Admiral Nelson) and then repeated the achievement a few years later with his film version of Noël Coward's play *Cavalcade* (1933).

Winning streak

When it comes to getting your hands on the coveted statuette, one man stands head and shoulders above everyone else. Walt Disney collected no fewer than 26 Academy Awards in his career, four of them honorary. He won his first Oscar in 1932 and his last, posthumously, in 1969. In all, he was nominated 59 times. It can only be hoped that his acceptance speeches were as animated as his cartoons.

Serial winners

Katharine Hepburn won a record four Best Actress awards in her long career, the last – for *On Golden Pond* in 1982 – coming almost 50 years after her first.

Jack Nicholson and Daniel Day-Lewis have three Oscars apiece (Nicholson's 12 nominations, eight for Best Actor, four for Best Supporting Actor, making him the most nominated male actor to date). In the late thirties, Walter Brennan, the garrulous and almost toothless (the result of an on-screen stunt that went wrong) character in countless Westerns, was a three-time winner in the Best Supporting Actor category. Meryl Streep picked up her third Oscar – putting her level with Ingrid Bergman – for her portrayal of Margaret Thatcher in *The Iron Lady* (2011). Streep's 18 nominations (15 for Best Actress, three for Best Supporting Actress) is an overall record.

In the Best Director category the American John Ford leads the way with four Oscars (plus two for wartime documentaries), though interestingly not one of them was for a Western, the genre for which he is best known. Veteran directors Frank Capra and William Wyler each carried off three awards. Heading the list of those who have won multiple awards for the same picture, each with three Oscars to his name, are:

Billy Wilder
The Apartment (1960):
Best Picture, Best Director, Best Original Screenplay

Francis Ford Coppola
The Godfather: Part II (1974):
Best Picture, Best Director, Best Adapted Screenplay

James L. Brooks
Terms of Endearment (1983):
Best Picture, Best Director, Best Adapted Screenplay

James Cameron
Titanic (1997):
Best Picture, Best Director, Best Film Editing

Peter Jackson
The Lord of the Rings: The Return of the King (2003):
Best Picture, Best Director, Best Adapted Screenplay

Joel and Ethan Coen
No Country for Old Men (2007):
Best Picture, Best Director, Best Adapted Screenplay

Alejandro González Iñárritu
Birdman (2014):
Best Picture, Best Director, Best Original Screenplay

Highs and lows

In 2003, The Lord of the Rings: The Return of the King *equalled the record of 11 Oscars, previously shared by* Ben-Hur *(1959) and* Titanic *(1997). Uniquely, the film won in every category for which it was nominated. Less successful were* The Turning Point *(1977) and* The Colour Purple *(1985), both of which received 11 nominations in their year but failed to muster a single award between them.*

Snubbing Oscar

The first person to reject an Oscar was the writer Dudley Nichols, whose screenplay for John Ford's *The Informer* – a story about the Irish troubles – earned him the award in 1936. At the time, screenwriters, along with some actors and directors, were trying to gain independence from the all-powerful studio system by establishing their own trade union. Boycotting the Awards ceremony was part of their campaign, though many got cold feet at the last moment and dutifully put in an appearance. But not Nichols, who not only shunned the event but when his Oscar was mailed to him later, returned it to the Academy.

It was no surprise that George C. Scott won the Best Actor award for his compelling performance in the title role of *Patton* in 1971. What did shock the assembled gathering was that he declined to turn up to collect it. But like the maverick US general he so memorably portrayed, the actor had a tendency to break ranks. Ten years before, Scott had refused a nomination for his supporting role in *The Hustler* (1961) and had described the Awards ceremony as a 'two-hour meat parade'. In 1972 he received yet another acting nomination, for the black comedy *The Hospital*. Few were surprised when the award went to someone more appreciative.

Message from the Godfather

Marlon Brando won his first Academy award for the 1954 movie *On the Waterfront*. His second, 19 years later, was for the role of Don Vito Corleone in Francis Ford Coppola's *The Godfather*. However, when Liv Ullmann (accompanied by Roger Moore) read out his name on the night, it was not Brando that arrived on stage but a young Apache actress and activist called Sacheen Littlefeather (real name Maria Cruz), wearing a Native American outfit. Clutching a lengthy prepared speech from Brando, which she promised to share with the media later, the eye-catching Ms Littlefeather proceeded to tell the stunned audience that the actor was rejecting the award because of the degrading portrayal of American Indians by the film and television industries. The message was delivered calmly and with dignity. The Godfather couldn't have done it better himself.

The Oscars: most nominations
(number of awards in brackets)

Best Director
William Wyler 12 (3)
Billy Wilder 8 (2)
Martin Scorsese 8 (1)
David Lean 7 (2)
Fred Zinnemann 7 (2)

Best Film
All About Eve (1950) 14 (6)
Titanic (1997) 14 (11)

Actor (Best and Supporting)
Jack Nicholson 12 (3)
Laurence Olivier 10 (1)
Paul Newman 10 (1)
Spencer Tracy 9 (2)

Actress (Best and Supporting)
Meryl Streep 18 (3)
Katharine Hepburn 12 (4)
Bette Davis 10 (2)
Geraldine Page 8 (1)

Other Categories
Walt Disney (animation) 59 (26), John Williams (music) 49 (5)
Cedric Gibbons (art direction) 39 (11), Edith Head (costume design) 35 (8)
Leon Shamroy (cinematography) 18 (4), Charles Lang (cinematography) 18 (1)
Woody Allen (original screenplay) 16 (3)

CHAPTER 10

ORIGINAL CASTING

Casting is a game of gut instinct. You feel their talent and potential in the pit of your stomach.

MARION DOUGHERTY, CASTING DIRECTOR

Some performances are so embedded in the psyche of the devoted movie fan that it is almost impossible to imagine anyone else in the role. Who but Humphrey Bogart could have played the romantically embittered Rick in *Casablanca* (1942)? Who other than Clint Eastwood could make our day as *Dirty Harry* (1971)? Yet neither actor was the studio's original choice.

The future president Ronald Reagan and George Raft, the coin-flipping star of the gangster movie *Scarface* (1932), were considered for the *Casablanca* part before Warner Brothers settled on Humphrey Bogart. Unhappy with the production once it was underway, both Bogart and his co-star Ingrid Bergman asked to be taken off the picture, but the studio insisted they fulfil their contracts. Luckily for us movie fans, they did.

Frank Sinatra was one of several stars (Steve McQueen and Paul Newman were others) offered the role of Inspector Harry Callahan in Warner Brothers' *Dirty Harry*. No doubt the studio had in mind Sinatra's tough-cop performance a couple of years earlier in the sexually frank thriller *The Detective* (the first Hollywood film in which the word 'semen' was uttered). But at 55, and with a fragile wrist, 'Ol' Blue Eyes' was not up to wielding a .44 Magnum.

Movie howler

In The Jewel of the Nile *(1985), the Nubian man who wrestles with Jack (Michael Douglas) in order to win Joan's (Kathleen Turner's) hand in marriage is wearing a conventional wedding ring – potentially adding bigamy to the charge sheet.*

Graduate studies

Crucial to Mike Nichols' 1967 film *The Graduate*, based on the novel of the same name, was the casting of the two central characters: the 20-year-old Benjamin Braddock, fresh down from university, and his would-be seductress, the 40-something Mrs Robinson. Robert Redford was initially the front runner for Benjamin, but Nichols wanted someone who would come across as being more vulnerable and less self-assured, and opted for an unknown Jewish actor named Dustin Hoffman.

High on the list of candidates to play Mrs Robinson was Ava Gardner, one of Hollywood's most famous screen sirens, but the actress promptly informed Nichols that she didn't take off her clothes for anybody. The part was then offered to Doris Day but, as she later recorded, she couldn't see herself rolling around in the sheets with someone half her age – fortunately, neither did we. Anne Bancroft, wife of Mel Brooks, made the part her own and earned an Oscar nomination.

Star caster

Under the old studio system typecasting was the name of the game. Producers drew actors from the studio's pool of contract players to fill all the roles in a movie (extras invariably came from the agency 'Central Casting' which was set up in 1925 to supply all the major studios with 'background talent'). Looks counted more than acting ability. Good guys were generally good-looking, bad girls were blonde and brassy. Actors were typecast as doctors, as business executives, as cab drivers or as landladies, appearing in similar roles in film after film – once a bad guy, always a bad guy. In British films it was the social class divisions, manifested by one's accent, which directed actors upstairs or downstairs.

One woman, more than anyone, changed the face of casting. Marion Dougherty set up a casting agency in New York in the early fifties, supplying actors for serious TV dramas, in those days filmed live. She searched for new talent off Broadway and among those she discovered were James Dean, Dustin Hoffman, Gene Hackman, Jon Voight, Al Pacino and Christopher Walken. Television's ambitious young directors, several of whom would go on to make it big in Hollywood, like John Frankenheimer (*Birdman of Alcatraz*, 1962), George Roy Hill (*Butch Cassidy and the Sundance Kid*, 1969) and Sidney Lumet (*Dog Day Afternoon*, 1975) were only too keen to showcase Dougherty's exciting new talent. Their work was transmitted coast to coast and there were those in Hollywood who began to sit up and take notice. Typecasting wouldn't disappear altogether, but it was no longer the only game in town.

Offbeat casting

Director Steven Spielberg prefers not to audition actors in the conventional way with a reading from the script. Instead he often assesses them by getting them to perform some trivial activity unrelated to the role. Actors lining up for Raiders of the Lost Ark *(1981) were ushered into the studio kitchen where they were asked to make cookies. To land her part in* Empire of the Sun *(1987), actress Emily Richard, who plays the young hero's mother, had to do nothing more than put up her hair for a moment, while Spielberg looked on.*

Desperately seeking Scarlett

From the moment producer David O. Selznick (he added the middle initial to give his name more distinction) bought the movie rights of Margaret Mitchell's bestselling novel *Gone with the Wind* in 1936, the hunt was on for an actress to play the heroine, Scarlett O'Hara. The media (skilfully manipulated by Selznick for publicity) joined in the search. Countless stars, starlets and unknown actresses were considered and discarded. Among the main contenders were Bette Davis, Katharine Hepburn and Paulette Goddard (at the time married to Charlie Chaplin and a neighbour of the Selznicks).

In December 1938 David O. Selznick, still without his Scarlett, embarked on the first scene to be shot – the burning of Atlanta (in reality the burning of many of the studio's old sets). According to the production schedule, there was little more than a month left in which to find his lead actress. Among those who turned up on the night to watch the fiery action was Selznick's brother Myron, a major Hollywood agent. He brought with him a relatively unknown English actress named Vivien Leigh, who was in California to see Laurence Olivier, with whom she was having an affair. Myron made the introductions to his brother: 'Hey, genius, here's your Scarlett O'Hara.' And it was.

Accident prone

Actress Halle Berry nearly choked on a fig during a sex scene with Pierce Brosnan in the James Bond movie, Die Another Day (2002). In her relatively short movie career Berry has broken an arm and a foot, damaged an eye and has twice been hospitalised with head injuries: a medical toll that is no doubt reflected in her insurance premiums.

Taking over

There are many instances of actors having to be replaced once shooting on a film has begun – and it has happened for a variety of reasons. Kim Basinger took over the role of Vicki Vale in *Batman* (1989) after the original choice, Sean Young, fell off a horse and broke her arm during rehearsals. Another casualty was Nicole Kidman, who had to leave the set of *Panic Room* (2002) after it was revealed that she had a hairline fracture in her knee, sustained while making *Moulin Rouge* the year before. Director David Fincher had wanted to shut down the production until his leading lady was fully fit, but the studio went ahead and recast with Jodie Foster. Song-and-dance man Buddy Ebsen was into his role of the Tin Man in *The Wizard of Oz* (1939) when he suffered a severe allergic reaction to the aluminium dust used in his make-up. He ended up in hospital and the more fortunate Jack Haley stepped into the part.

Sometimes actors are replaced because the director changes his mind. Four weeks into shooting *Back to the Future* (1985), director Robert Zemeckis decided that Eric Stoltz had been miscast in the role of Marty McFly and substituted Michael J. Fox. Fellow director Peter Jackson was quicker off the mark, concluding on the first day of *The Lord of the Rings: The Fellowship of the Ring* (2001) that Stuart Townsend was too young to play Aragorn. Viggo Mortensen landed the part for the entire trilogy.

On a more sombre note, John Candy, Oliver Reed and Heath Ledger are among those who, in relatively recent times, have died mid-film. In 1958, Hollywood star Tyrone Power was making *Solomon and Sheba* in Rome, under the direction of King Vidor. Power, who had completed most of his scenes on the movie, was filming a vigorous swordfight with co-star George Sanders when he collapsed with a heart attack. He died en route to the hospital, aged 44. Yul Brynner was brought in to re-shoot the part of Solomon, though Tyrone Power can still be glimpsed in some of the long shots.

Stung by Cleopatra

Casting Elizabeth Taylor in the title role of *Cleopatra* (1963) almost brought Twentieth Century Fox to its knees. The studio had pencilled in Joan Collins, who was already under contract to them, but the film's producer Walter Wanger held out for Taylor and the studio eventually caved in. The actress asked for $1 million – an unprecedented fee in those days. She also insisted that the film be shot using the expensive 70 mm Todd-AO system pioneered by her late husband, Mike Todd. Wanger agreed to everything.

Despite the problematic British climate and the Egyptian–Roman setting, it was decided to shoot the film at Pinewood Studios in England. Peter Finch and Stephen Boyd were cast as Caesar and Antony respectively, and the budget was upwardly adjusted from $2 million to $5 million.

Bad weather and a constantly ill Elizabeth Taylor delayed filming. Meanwhile Taylor's then husband, the singer Eddie Fisher, was being paid $150,000 to be her minder. When the actress contracted double pneumonia and almost died, the production was shut down for six months. Peter Finch and Stephen Boyd pulled out of the film to meet other commitments, with Rex Harrison and Richard Burton taking over their roles. Joseph Mankiewicz replaced Rouben Mamoulian as director, and the production shifted to Rome. The budget soared.

Elizabeth Taylor began her much-publicised affair with Richard Burton, and there were further costly delays as the actress gave way to stress and assorted bouts of ill health. Filming finally came to an end 29 months after it had begun. The final cost of the movie was $44 million – at today's values around $339 million. Elizabeth Taylor's fee ultimately came out at $7 million (some $46 million today).

What might have been: famous roles that nearly went to other actors

Midnight Cowboy (1969)
Joe Buck

Michael Sarrazin	Jon Voight

Alien (1979)
Ripley

Meryl Streep	Sigourney Weaver

Apocalypse Now (1979)
Captain Willard

Steve McQueen	Martin Sheen

Raiders of the Lost Ark (1981)
Indiana Jones

Tom Selleck	Harrison Ford

Hook (1991)
Captain Hook

David Bowie	Dustin Hoffman

Batman Returns (1992)
Catwoman

Annette Bening	Michelle Pfeiffer

Forrest Gump (1994)
Forrest Gump

John Travolta	Tom Hanks

The Matrix (1999)
Neo

Will Smith	Keanu Reeves

The Lord of the Rings (2001)
Gandalf

Sean Connery	Ian McKellen

Harry Potter and the Sorcerer's Stone (2001)
Rubeus Hagrid

Robin Williams	Robbie Coltrane

	offered to		played by

CHAPTER 11

BUCKING THE SYSTEM

I'm not a Hollywood director. I'm an in-spite-of-Hollywood director.
MARTIN SCORSESE

In 1948 the US Supreme Court ordered seven Hollywood studios to divest themselves of their cinema networks (which only showed films produced by the studios that owned them), thus separating production and distribution and breaking the industry's monopoly. Television began to take its toll on cinema audience numbers, a process that would accelerate throughout the 1950s. By the start of the seventies the movie business was in freefall and the weekly cinema audience was down to 15 million from a high of 78 million in 1946.

Rebels with a cause

A cultural revolution was underway in America and elsewhere in the western world. Young people had little interest in the films produced by the studios. It was the time of anti-Vietnam War protests, of drugs and sexual liberation, of student riots and Black Power. It was the age of the anti-hero. Old-timers like John Wayne, Gary Cooper and Henry Fonda gave way to newcomers like Jack Nicholson, Robert De Niro and Al Pacino.

A new wave of young film-makers was in town, determined to break with Hollywood convention. They used new techniques to make their low-budget movies. Hand-held cameras, natural sound and the cheaper 16 mm film stock (instead of the usual 35 mm) became commonplace. Dennis Hopper's 1969 biker movie, *Easy Rider*, starring himself and Peter Fonda and introducing Jack Nicholson, was a runaway success and is seen as a watershed. The new permissiveness was luring people away from the blander fare on television. Cinema and its young warriors were fighting back.

President Rambo

Commenting on the successful resolution to the hijacking of a TWA plane at Beirut Airport in 1985, President Reagan was quoted as saying: 'Boy, I'm glad I saw Rambo *last night. Now I'll know what to do next time.'*

Milestone movies

Some new directors were making their films with studio backing, others sourced the finance elsewhere, but all strove to maintain independent control of their projects. Between them they made the seventies one of cinema's most creative decades, pushing back the frontiers of film-making and revitalising the industry in the process. Movies changed in content as much as in style. Subjects that had been ignored or sidestepped by the big studios now took centre stage. Sex, drugs, mindless violence, disaffected youth and a dirty war became the stuff of cinema. Four-letter words became as familiar on the screen as they were in everyday life. The dream factory was getting real, and not before time.

Not all the new films were shocking or downbeat (though enough of them were), but the best of them were edgy and exciting and had something to say, and they changed the face of cinema. Jerry Schatzberg's documentary-style movie about a heroin addict, *The Panic in Needle Park* (1971), introduced Al Pacino to the screen (competing for the same role had been the equally unknown Robert De Niro). Peter Bogdanovich's *The Last Picture Show* (1972), filmed in black and white, is an evocatively bleak look at small-town America in the fifties. Hal Ashby's *The Last Detail* (1973) is a salty comedy drama about a Navy shore patrol. Terrence Malick's *Badlands* (1973) sends a beguilingly youthful Martin Sheen and Sissy Spacek on a state-to-state killing spree. Milos Foreman's *One Flew Over the Cuckoo's Nest* (1975) finds humour in a mental institution and earned Jack Nicholson his first Oscar. The *annus mirabilis* of 1977 gave the world George Lucas's *Star Wars* and Steven Spielberg's *Close Encounters of the Third Kind*.

William Friedkin reinvented the car chase (just as *Bullitt* had done a few years earlier) in *The French Connection* (1971). George Roy Hill's *The Sting* (1973) reunited Paul Newman and Robert Redford. Three disturbing films examined the scarring after-effects of the Vietnam War: Martin Scorsese's *Taxi Driver* (1976), Michael Cimino's *The Deer Hunter* (1978) and Francis Ford Coppola's *Apocalypse Now* (1979). With the shackles of censorship well and truly loosened came Stanley Kubrick's thuggishly violent *A Clockwork Orange* (1971), Mike Nichols' sexually probing *Carnal Knowledge* (1971) and Italian director Bernardo Bertolucci's erotically charged *Last Tango in Paris* (1972).

It was also the decade of *The Godfather* (1972) and *Mean Streets* (1973), of *American Graffiti* (1973) and *Jaws* (1975).

The Godfather

If Paramount Pictures thought that hiring the young Francis Ford Coppola to direct the movie version of Mario Puzo's bestselling novel would enable them to control the project, they were very much mistaken. The 31-year-old Coppola's previous movies had shown an original film-maker at work but had performed only modestly at the box office. Handing him *The Godfather* was a gamble but from the outset the independently minded Coppola made the movie his own (though for a while the studio kept another director in reserve, just in case Coppola bombed out).

There were constant battles with the management. Paramount wanted to set the story in modern-day Kansas City; Coppola insisted on making it 1940s New York, as in the novel. The studio didn't want Al Pacino as Michael Corleone (the actor made four screen tests, all of which were rejected by Paramount) or Diane Keaton as his wife (too uncharismatic, too tall); but most of all they didn't want Marlon Brando, who was considered too much of a handful on the set.

The Mafia had been persuaded to back off having initially threatened to close down the production. Now Coppola tried some persuasion of his own. He shot some trial footage of Brando, the actor's cheeks stuffed with Kleenex, his eyes shadowed with shoe polish, his voice a rasping distortion, and showed it to Paramount. It proved to be an offer the studio couldn't refuse.

Mean Streets

Martin Scorsese originally intended to become a priest but, happily for movie fans, he switched vocations. While still a student at New York University's film school he made several prizewinning shorts, before trying his luck in Hollywood where he worked as an editor and assistant director. He joined the ranks of fellow 'movie brats', Coppola, Spielberg, Lucas and Brian De Palma.

In 1972 Scorsese made *Boxcar Bertha*, a violent but generally undistinguished film set in the Depression era. His next project was to be closer to home. *Mean Streets* follows the fortunes of two friends in the criminal underworld of Manhattan's Little Italy, where Scorsese grew up. The low-budget, independently financed production helped launch the careers of Robert De Niro and Harvey Keitel, who play the two friends. Scorsese drew on his own background for some of the story material, the feckless De Niro character being partly based on the director's uncle who was always in trouble.

The movie, shot in a month, was a critical success. As well as being violent, it realistically features a lot of bad language, in particular the F-word. After watching the film a somewhat shocked Mrs Scorsese, the director's mother, commented: 'We *never* used that word in the house.'

American Graffiti

George Lucas's nostalgic coming-of-age movie also referenced the director's personal background, though in an altogether more wholesome way than *Mean Streets*. Set in a small Californian town (similar to the one in which Lucas himself grew up) in 1962, it predates Vietnam and the drug scene. The relatively innocent preoccupations of the teenage group of high-school graduate friends were far removed from those of the film's audience, who turned up in their millions to see it and to hear its soundtrack of rock 'n' roll hits of the era.

The little-known cast included the up-and-coming Richard Dreyfus, Harrison Ford and Ron Howard who, carrying on from his role in TV's *Happy Days*, eventually became a distinguished director himself. Despite *American Graffiti*'s huge financial success (Lucas's friend Coppola had produced the film), the director found it hard to get his next project, *Star Wars*, off the ground. Universal, his incumbent studio, turned it down and Lucas (taking Harrison Ford with him) moved on to Twentieth Century Fox. Although it went over budget, *Star Wars* still came out at a manageable $11 million. Lucas shrewdly negotiated to hang on to the merchandising rights, not at the time thought to be worth very much. He's still counting the money.

Jaws

As a child, Steven Spielberg staged train crashes on his model railway and filmed them with his father's 8 mm camera. It was good practice for what was to follow. After an apprenticeship in television, Spielberg had critical success with his first two feature films, *Duel* (1972), originally made for TV, and *The Sugarland Express* (1973); but *Jaws*, based on Peter Benchley's bestselling novel about a man-eating shark terrorising an East Coast summer resort, was on an altogether different scale.

One of Spielberg's principal concerns was the shark itself. Reluctantly he accepted that a mechanical version of the creature would have to be used, since they could hardly hope to tame or train an actual Great White. However, the success of the film would stand or fall on the credibility of what was produced. Bob Mattey, who had created the giant squid that attacks the *Nautilus* in the 1954 film *20,000 Leagues Under the Sea*, was brought out of retirement to do the job.

Nicknamed 'Bruce', Mattey's polyurethane shark weighed 1.5 tonnes and required a crew of 13 to operate it. Three identical models were produced as back ups. The shark needed constant maintenance to protect it from the ravages of the sea (it also frequently malfunctioned) and was kept under wraps to conceal it from the media and prying public. In the event, 'Bruce' did a terrifyingly good job. Within a fortnight of its release, the movie had grossed three times its outlay of $8 million.

> ### Rising scale
>
> Al Pacino received a modest $35,000 for his role in The Godfather (1972). For The Godfather: Part II (1974) the actor's fee rose to $500,000, plus ten per cent of the gross after break-even. For part III of the series, 16 years later, he was on a cool $5 million.

Being independent

The distinction between the independent film-maker and the big studio is not always easy to define. Some studios have an independent arm that underwrites developing talent. Some of the distribution companies that finance independent films are themselves owned by studios. Producers and directors flitter from one to the other, chasing the money. At the end of the day, nothing counts more than getting the work up there on the big screen.

Whatever the complexity of the financing, the independent sector is a nursery for new ideas and new talent. Subjects that studios would normally shun (at least under their own name) can be explored by the independent filmmaker. Actors can go out on a limb, or play against type – or if they have George Clooney's clout, make their own movies. A low budget can sometimes be liberating.

The seventies paved the way for film-makers like Quentin Tarantino, Steven Soderbergh, Jane Campion, the Coen brothers, David Fincher, Kathryn Bigelow, Danny Boyle and others around the world. Tucked away in New York, and always keeping himself free to play jazz on Monday nights, the prolific Woody Allen has proved the most enduring and independent of them all.

Rambo: the body count

[These figures (from the *Los Angeles Times*, 2008) include those killed by firearm, bow and arrow, knife, grenade, rocket launcher and with bare hands, both on the ground and from the air – just over half of them despatched by Rambo himself. Not included are the multiple victims of attacks on buildings, tanks, trucks, helicopters and the like, where the number wiped out is unquantifiable.]

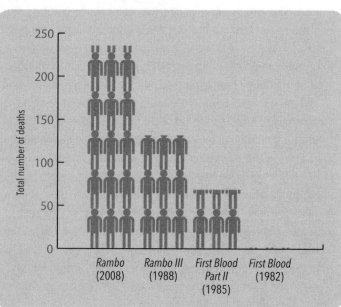

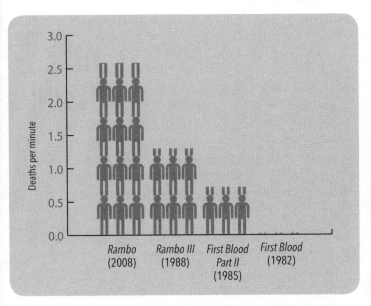

Deaths per minute

3.0
2.5
2.0
1.5
1.0
0.5
0.0

Rambo (2008) — Rambo III (1988) — First Blood Part II (1985) — First Blood (1982)

Movie howler

In the 2001 version of Ocean's Eleven, *directed by Steven Soderbergh, Rusty (Brad Pitt) is seen holding a shrimp cup whilst in conversation with Linus (Matt Damon). As the scene progresses the cup is mysteriously replaced by a plate, only to return to being a cup once again before they finish chatting.*

CHAPTER 12

AND...
ACTION!

*A film is never really good unless the camera
is an eye in the head of a poet.*

ORSON WELLES, ACTOR AND DIRECTOR

In the first tentative years of film-making it was the person operating the camera who directed the action. As movies became more advanced the role of the film director evolved. Under the old Hollywood studio system directors under contract would be assigned movies, much as the stars were. Some directors, like the actors themselves, became typecast and associated with a particular movie genre. George Cukor, who directed Katharine Hepburn in some of her most successful films, developed a reputation as a 'woman's director', though he also elicited memorable performances from several male stars. Originally chosen by David O. Selznick to direct *Gone with the Wind*, Cukor was forced off the film by Clark Gable who felt that the director was giving too much attention to his female co-star Vivien Leigh.

The *auteur* theory, in which the director is viewed as the major creative influence on a film (in effect the 'author' of it) took root in France in the 1950s and was applied to film-makers like Alfred Hitchcock and Ingmar Bergman who stamped their style on every movie they made. Many modern directors – from Mike Leigh to Woody Allen – fall into this category, their films reflecting a personal creative vision that goes far beyond simply directing actors on a set.

Female of the species

There are several high-profile female directors making movies today – Claire Denis (35 Shots of Rum, 2008), Catherine Hardwicke (Twilight, 2008), Jane Campion (Bright Star, 2009), Phyllida Lloyd (The Iron Lady, 2011), Kathryn Bigelow (Zero Dark Thirty, 2012) and Sofia Coppola (The Bling Ring, 2013), to name but a few. However, for a number of years during the Hollywood boom period of the thirties and forties, only one woman got to yell 'Action'. Dorothy Arzner started out as a studio stenographer and worked her way through the editing department before being given a chance to direct in 1927. Her dozen or so movies were mainly social comedies, with a strong female bias in the storylines, but with all that male prejudice around, who could blame her?

Legendary directors

Here are ten of the most influential film-makers of world cinema.

Ingmar Bergman (1918-2007)

Born in Sweden, the son of a Lutheran minister, Bergman had a severely repressed childhood, which probably accounts for much of the angst that characterises his films. His work makes challenging viewing, often tackling subjects like madness, despair and death that other film-makers avoided. In one of his most famous films, *The Seventh Seal* (1957), Death is physically portrayed as one of the leading characters. Bergman, who also wrote and directed many theatre productions, had complete control over his films from script to final edit. He worked mainly with the same small coterie of actors, among them Liv Ullman, Bibi Andersson, Harriet Andersson (the five-times-married Bergman had affairs with all three and Ullman bore his child) and Max Von Sydow. His best-known films include *Smiles of a Summer Night* (1955), *Wild Strawberries* (1957), *The Virgin Spring* (1960) and *Cries and Whispers* (1972).

Luis Buñuel (1900-1983)

The great Spanish director's first film was a deliberately shocking affair. Made in collaboration with fellow surrealist (the cultural movement that had started in Paris in the early twenties) and friend from his student days, the artist Salvador Dalí, *Un Chien Andalou* (*An Andalusian Dog*, 1928) is a 16-minute series of dream-like images designed to startle the audience. One of the earlier sequences is that of a woman's eyeball being sliced open with a straight razor. Buñuel's films were revolutionary in style and content, the Catholic Church and affluent middle classes often the target of his savage satire. He was based for long periods of time in France, Mexico and his native Spain, making films in several languages. Among his most celebrated movies are *The Diary of a Chambermaid* (1960), *Belle de Jour* (1967), *Tristana* (1970) and *The Discreet Charm of the Bourgeoisie* (1972).

Federico Fellini (1920-1993)

Fellini emerged from the post-war movement in Italian film-making known as neorealism – movies that focused on the harsh realities of contemporary life, shot in documentary style and often using non-professional actors. Roberto Rossellini, Vittorio De Sica and Luchino Visconti were other eminent directors who made films in this style. Fellini's *La Strada* (*The Road*, 1956), a touching tale of three fatally flawed performers in a small itinerant circus travelling through the impoverished wasteland of post-war Italy, brought him the first of four Oscars for Best Foreign Language Film. The film starred the director's wife, Giulietta Masina, who appeared in several of his movies. After *La Dolce*

Vita (*The Sweet Life*, 1959), *8½* (1963) and *Juliet of the Spirits* (1965), Fellini's films became more esoteric and self-indulgent, frequently leaving audiences stranded in their wake.

Howard Hawks (1896-1977)

Howard Hawks made movies about tough men and wise-cracking women. He made his mark with *The Dawn Patrol* (1930), a World War Two film with some impressive flying sequences (Hawks himself had been a wartime pilot). Two years later came the original *Scarface*, with Paul Muni in the title role. Over the next four decades Hawks directed screwball comedies such as *Bringing Up Baby* (1938), *His Girl Friday* (1940) and *Monkey Business* (1952) – all starring Cary Grant – as well as action dramas like *Only Angels Have Wings* (1939), *Sergeant York* (1941) and *To Have and Have Not* (1944), which brought together Humphrey Bogart and the 19-year-old Lauren Bacall. The couple, now married, co-starred in Hawks's next film, *The Big Sleep* (1946). The 1953 musical *Gentlemen Prefer Blondes* featured two of Hollywood's best-known bust measurements, in the form of Jane Russell and Marilyn Monroe. And then there were the classic John Wayne Westerns, *Red River* (1947) and *Rio Bravo* (1958) – some CV.

Alfred Hitchcock (1899-1980)

Referring to his cinema audience in an interview, the 'Master of Suspense' once said: 'I'm more scared than they are of things in real life.' Understanding his own fears helped Hitchcock to create nail-biting tension on screen. Wordless sequences are used to build up terror as, for example, in *Psycho* (1960) when Martin

Balsam as the detective climbs the stairs that lead to his death, or in *The Birds* (1963) when the crows menacingly assemble in the school playground as the children sing inside. Not the least remarkable aspect of Hitchcock's film-making was that he never needed to look through the camera – every shot was planned and framed in his mind before shooting got underway. After a series of box-office successes in the UK during the 1930s, he moved to America and won an Oscar (Best Picture) for his first film there, *Rebecca* (1940). Some 30 thrillers followed, most of them gripping and many demonstrating the portly director's voyeuristic penchant for blondes.

Akira Kurosawa (1910–1998)

Akira Kurosawa remains Japan's most influential director outside his native land. He achieved international recognition with *Rashomon* (1950), which won the top prize at the Venice Film Festival and was later remade in Hollywood as a western (*The Outrage*, 1964). Kurosawa's idol was the American director John Ford, but others equally admired the Japanese film-maker. *The Magnificent Seven* was John Sturges's version of Kurosawa's *Seven Samurai* (1954), Sergio Leone's *A Fistful of Dollars* was based on *Yokimbo* (1961) and George Lucas's *Star Wars: Episode IV – A New Hope* owes much to Kurosawa's 1958 classic, *The Hidden Fortress*. Two of his finest films are adaptations of Shakespearean plays: *Throne of Blood* (1957) is his take on *Macbeth* and *Ran* (1985) is an epic retelling of *King Lear*. In 1970, his career at a low ebb, Kurosawa attempted suicide. He failed and continued making movies for another 20 years.

F. W. Murnau (1888-1931)

The films of F. W. Murnau (real name Friedrich Wilhelm Plumpe) are associated with the 1920s cultural movement known as German expressionism, characterised in the movies of the time by highly stylised set designs, strange camera angles and shadowy lighting effects. Murnau's most famous work is *Nosferatu* (1922), based on Bram Stoker's nineteenth-century novel *Dracula*. Aptly subtitled *A Symphony of Terror*, the film is widely regarded as the ultimate horror movie. When permission to film the book was refused, the studio just changed the name – Count Dracula became Count Orlok and 'Nosferatu' simply means vampire. Stoker's heirs won a subsequent court action against the studio, which was forced to destroy all prints of the film – save one. In 1927 Murnau moved to America where he made another masterpiece, *Sunrise*: *A Song of Two Humans*. The film was critically acclaimed but a box-office disaster. Four years later Murnau died in a car accident.

Satyajit Ray (1921-1992)

The Indian director Satyajit Ray's first feature film, *Pather Panchali* (1955), established his reputation overnight, achieving 11 international awards. Beautifully shot and paced, the film depicts the challenging childhood of Apu and his sister in their impoverished Bengali village. Ray (pronounced 'rye') went on to make two more films about his central character, creating what has become known as the 'Apu Trilogy'. He was the complete *auteur*, writing the screenplays for his films as well as editing them and more often than not composing the music. The multifaceted film-maker also wrote detective novels and children's stories, a number of which he successfully adapted for the screen. His fellow director Akira Kurosawa said of his work: 'To have not seen the films of Ray is to have lived in the world without ever having seen the moon and the sun.'

Jean Renoir (1894–1979)

Son of the French impressionist painter Pierre-Auguste Renoir, Jean Renoir made a number of silent movies during the twenties, several of them starring his wife Catherine Hessling – his father's last model. In 1937 came his magnum opus, *La grande illusion* (*The Great Illusion*), an anti-war film with Jean Gabin and the German actor–director Erich von Stroheim. It was followed two years later by *La règle du jeu* (*The Rules of the Game*), a brilliant satire on the French upper classes, with Renoir himself playing the central character. The French public hated the film and the government banned it. Mercifully the film was resurrected during the fifties and is now recognised as a classic of world cinema. Renoir made several films in Hollywood, the best of which is *The Southerner* (1945), a story about Texas sharecroppers. Of his later work, *The River* (1951), shot in India and his first in colour, and the charmingly energetic *French Cancan* (1954), stand out.

Orson Welles (1915–1985)

Most film critics place *Citizen Kane* (1941) at the top of their lists of all-time greats. However, what makes this dazzling, groundbreaking film even more remarkable is that it was Orson Welles' debut as a movie actor and director. Aided and abetted by cinematographer Gregg Toland and Herman J. Mankiewicz, who co-wrote the screenplay, the young genius put down a new marker in the art of film-making. His next film, *The Magnificent Ambersons* (1942), about the declining fortunes of a family at the turn of the twentieth century, is close to being another masterpiece. After that it was Welles' own career that was in decline. *The Lady from Shanghai* (1947) and *Touch of Evil* (1958), both directed by and co-starring Welles, are fine films and there are occasional flashes of directorial brilliance in some of his other works. But as Orson Welles himself put it: 'I started at the top and worked my way down.'

Top ten countries at the box office (2013)

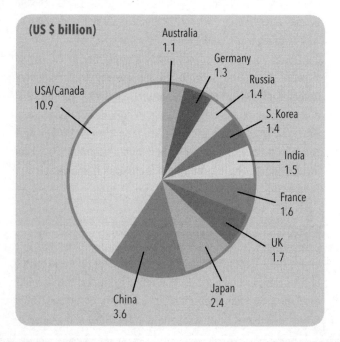

(US $ billion)

Australia 1.1
Germany 1.3
Russia 1.4
S. Korea 1.4
India 1.5
France 1.6
UK 1.7
Japan 2.4
China 3.6
USA/Canada 10.9

Critical mass

The 'New Wave' ('Nouvelle vague') movement in French cinema during the late fifties and sixties was led by a group of former film critics. François Truffaut, Jean-Luc Godard, Eric Rohmer and Claude Chabrol were regular contributors to the influential movie magazine Cahiers du Cinéma ('Notebooks on Cinema'), sitting in judgement on other people's films before themselves becoming internationally acclaimed directors. Love and social alienation are recurring themes in their work which in general rejected the traditional narrative techniques of French cinema in favour of a more radical style that made greater use of symbolism and abstraction. Among their best-known films are Godard's À bout de souffle (Breathless, 1960), Truffaut's Jules et Jim (Jules and Jim, 1962), Rohmer's Ma nuit chez Maude (My Night with Maude, 1969) and Chabrol's Le boucher (The Butcher, 1970).

Ten European film-makers to check out

Director: Paul Greengrass
Keynote film: *Bloody Sunday* (2002)

Director: Lynne Ramsay
Keynote film: *We Need to Talk About Kevin* (2011)

Director: Michael Winterbottom
Keynote film: *Welcome to Sarajevo* (1997)

Director: Alexander Sokurov
Keynote film: *Faust* (2011)

Director: Lars von Trier
Keynote film: *Melancholia* (2011)

Director: Werner Herzog
Keynote film: *Fitzcarraldo* (1982)

Director: Claire Denis
Keynote film: *Chocolat* (1988)

Director: Jacques Audiard
Keynote film: *A Prophet* (2009)

Director: Michael Haneke
Keynote film: *The White Ribbon* (2009)

Director: Pedro Almodóvar
Keynote film: *All About My Mother* (1999)

CHAPTER 13

COMING ATTRACTIONS

I can't stand digital film-making – it's TV in public.

QUENTIN TARANTINO, DIRECTOR

Cinema continues to astound. At the 2012 Academy Awards, the Oscar for Best Picture went to Michel Hazanavicius's *The Artist*. It was the first French film to receive the award, but what was even more surprising was that the movie was silent and in black and white (it was actually shot in colour, in just 35 days, but with the styling and techniques of the silent era). The last silent film to be voted Best Picture had been William Wellman's *Wings*, at the inaugural ceremony in 1929.

The following year saw the release of the Mexican director Alfonso Cuarón's sci-fi thriller *Gravity*. The two films could hardly be more different. Eighty per cent of the 91-minute-long space drama consists of computer graphics (this compares with 60 per cent of *Avatar*), the stunning visual effects the culmination of three years' work by the London-based company Framestore. Sandra Bullock and George Clooney are the stars (the original choices were Natalie Portman and Robert Downey Jr), but it is the spectacular computer-generated images of outer space that catch the eye. If *The Artist* is an affectionate look back at how films used to be made, *Gravity* is a sign of things to come.

Hooray for Bollywood

Bollywood has become synonymous with the Indian film industry though in fact it produces only a quarter of India's annual output of some 1,200 movies – twice the number made in Hollywood. Centred around Mumbai (formerly Bombay, hence 'Bollywood', a name bestowed on the film-making community in the 1970s) it primarily makes films in the Hindi language.

Song and dance are often essential components of the typical Bollywood film. Overt sex is seldom on view and until recently kissing, especially the open-mouthed variety, was strictly taboo. Bollywood and Hollywood are getting together more and more with actors, directors and musicians – along with the ubiquitous moneymen – crossing the cultural divide. Naturally there are considerable financial rewards to be had from such collaborations – but that's Bollywood for you.

Motion capture performance

When, in 1999, Andy Serkis's agent offered him three weeks' work doing the voice for an animated character in a new movie, the actor asked if he couldn't be found a proper role. The film was the first in *The Lord of the Rings* trilogy and the character in search of a voice was Gollum. Serkis was so successful in getting under the skin of the slimy ex-Hobbit, despite never having read the book, that director Peter Jackson subsequently cast him in the more vertically challenging role of King Kong in the 2005 remake. Since then Serkis has become cinema's most accomplished actor in performance-capture roles, with an impressive list of credits that includes the simian Caesar in two recent *Planet of the Apes* movies and an uncharacteristically Scottish-sounding Captain Haddock in Spielberg's *The Adventures of Tintin* (2011).

Performance-capture skills and technology are changing the face of fantasy movies in particular. The actor creates the physical, emotional and psychological aspects of the character as for any conventional part. This live-action performance – for which the actor, instead of wearing costume and make-up, dons a Lycra bodysuit studded with reflective markers – is then translated into a digital one, the three-dimensional avatar mirroring the actor's characterisation. Tucked away in the old Ealing Studios in West London, home to many famous British films of the post-war era, is 'The Imaginarium', a creative digital studio co-founded by Andy Serkis that is taking motion capture performance to new levels. There is, it would seem, virtually no limit.

Digital v celluloid

The advent of digital technology has seriously undermined the future of celluloid film. The industry is divided on the issue, with many top directors and cinematographers having opposing views. Filming on celluloid is a costly, wasteful and time-consuming business. Each reel produces just ten minutes of footage, so the reel has to be constantly changed. The material 'in the can' is developed overnight, which means that the director and others don't get to see the results of their work until the following day (the so-called 'rushes' or 'dailies'). Only then do they discover if anything needs to be re-shot, with potential knock-on problems such as weather, schedule and availability of actors, not to mention cost.

There are no such impediments with the digital process. Not having to worry about burning up the budget on expensive film stock, directors can afford to keep the camera running. Furthermore, they can view the recorded action on the spot. All this provides more scope for improvisation and experimentation. The availability of relatively cheap, high-quality digital cameras that are compact and mobile has opened up the market for aspiring film-makers, though advances in technology can never be a substitute for talent. On the other side of the argument, advocates of celluloid claim that digital reproduction cannot match the subtle texturing and aesthetic appeal of film – though this may escape the average viewer. As technology continues to develop and existing systems become outmoded, there are concerns that the long-term preservation of many digital movies will be in jeopardy. (Ironically, celluloid movies too are threatened with extinction if projection equipment becomes obsolete – unless, that is, they are transferred to digital form.)

Taking sides

Believing that the future is digital, some manufacturers have stopped making traditional movie cameras and have cut back on the production of film stock. Although the battle is not yet over, there can be little doubt that the next generation of film-makers will overwhelmingly favour digital, if only because they will have grown up with it. Several major directors who made their name working with celluloid film are now firmly in the digital camp, among them James Cameron (*Avatar*, 2009), David Fincher (*The Girl with the Dragon Tattoo*, 2011), David Lynch (*Inland Empire*, 2006) and Danny Boyle – whose 2002 post-apocalyptic horror film *28 Days Later* was the first mainstream movie to be shot in digital form. (Seven years later his multi-award-winning *Slumdog Millionaire* became the first digitally shot movie to win an Oscar for cinematography.)

Quentin Tarantino (*Django Unchained*, 2012), Paul Thomas Anderson (*The Master*, 2012) and the British director Christopher Nolan (*Interstellar*, 2014) have all come out on the side of film. Martin Scorsese has been another staunch defender of celluloid, despite having made the gloriously three-dimensional *Hugo* in 2011. When it came to his next movie, *The Wolf of Wall Street* (2013), Scorsese reluctantly compromised, shooting most of it on film but with some sequences shot with a digital camera.

The way ahead

The digital revolution has helped democratise film-making, the small independent operator feeding off the same technology that drives the annual studio blockbuster. Just about anyone these days can make a movie, shooting on the streets or in the local park and editing on the computer. Whether, at the professional level, a finished film gets to be seen (or even made in the first place) ultimately depends on landing a distribution deal. There is a permanent bottleneck when it comes to distribution on both sides of the Atlantic with the big studios and in-demand film-makers inevitably jumping the queue. As Orson Welles once summed up the business: 'It's about two per cent movie-making and 98 per cent hustling.' This is an equation that is unlikely to change.

Just as in the 1950s, when television made damaging inroads into the traditional movie audience, the challenge is to attract more people into the cinema. Sixty years ago the studios fought back with 3D, widescreen and multitrack sound – Cinerama, CinemaScope, VistaVision and Todd-AO (which used 70 mm film as opposed to the standard 35 mm to achieve enhanced definition). Some initiatives were more successful than others but collectively they helped reverse the trend; at least for a time. Multiscreens aside, cinemas have not fundamentally changed since the thirties (though many have swapped their ornate décor for a more bleakly functional style). If they are to start packing in the patrons – and keep abreast of the technically groundbreaking films they show – exhibitors will need to create a movie-going experience that outstrips the advances in home entertainment. Enhanced presentation systems like 4D, with simulated effects (movement, smell, mist, etc.) to augment the on-screen action, could one day be coming to a cinema near you.

Cinema verities

Some things are unlikely to change. The James Bond franchise (a word that has crept into cinema's vocabulary in recent years) spans 24 films and more than 50 years, the 007 character refreshed by the latest incumbent, Daniel Craig. No other movie series has lasted as long and, like *The Mousetrap* on the London stage, it seems set to run and run.

Courtesy of TV's movie channels and more especially DVDs, we can revisit favourite films or plunder the archives in search of unknown treasures. Some 90 per cent of silent films have gone forever, but those that have been preserved and restored make rewarding viewing. New films will continue to entertain, inform and surprise – and, on occasion, disappoint. Some will have that elusive ingredient that turns a modest production into a global success – like *Four Weddings and a Funeral* (1994), *The Blair Witch Project* (1999) and *The King's Speech* (2010). Others will reach the heights because of the troubling integrity of the story told, as with Steven Spielberg's *Schindler's List* (1993) and Steve McQueen's *12 Years a Slave* (2013).

Cinema probes every corner of our existence as well as revealing worlds of pure invention. It is energising, transporting and cathartic. It can make us laugh or cry, sing and dance, shriek in terror or sit open-mouthed with astonishment. There are heroes to revere and villains to revile. Our own anxieties and problems are put on hold while we share those of the characters on screen. Illusion takes over from reality, and for a while sometimes we can't tell the difference between the two.

That's the magic of cinema – and the joy.

CHAPTER 14

GLOSSARY OF MOVIE TERMS

Best boy Assistant to the head electrician ('best boy electric') or head grip ('best boy grip').

Bridging shot A shot inserted to cover a jump in time or place, e.g. turning calendar pages or speeding train wheels.

Cinematographer The person in charge of the camera and lighting crew, usually referred to as Director of Photography.

Cinéma-vérité 'Cinema of truth': a documentary style of film-making that began in France in the 1950s, showing people in everyday situations and using authentic dialogue etc.

CGI Computer-generated imagery.

Cross-cutting Cutting between different sets of action, typically to build suspense or to establish a link between activities.

Deep focus A technique that enables objects close to the camera and those further away to be simultaneously in focus.

Dolly Wheeled platform on which the camera is mounted.

Film noir Term used to describe a genre of American film dramas, mainly from the 1940s and 1950s, with bleak storylines and hardbitten characters.

Footage The length of a film measured in feet; 90 feet equals approximately one minute of running time.

Frame Single image. There are 16 frames per foot of 35 mm film, with most films shot at a speed of 24 frames a second.

Gaffer Head electrician.

Grip Man in charge of the camera rigging and of operating camera cranes and dollies etc.

Jump cut An abrupt cut between two sequential shots that compresses time and by its suddenness draws attention to the action.

MacGuffin A plot device that advances the story and motivates the characters but has no particular significance beyond that, e.g. the Rabbit's Foot in *Mission: Impossible III* (2006). The term was often used by Alfred Hitchcock.

Matte shot A shot in which the background and/or foreground are masked to enable different images to be substituted later.

Mise-en-scène The artistic elements that contribute to the staging of a shot or scene, such as props, costumes, lighting, camera angles (literally: 'putting in the scene').

Montage A series of short shots edited into a sequence to condense space, time and information.

Slate Another name for a clapperboard.

Stop-motion animation Clay or plasticine models that are physically manipulated and photographed frame by frame, to create the effect of movement.

Take A scene of any length filmed without stopping the camera.

Voice-over The voice of a narrator or on-screen character not seen speaking.

If you're interested in finding out more about our books, find us on Facebook at **Summersdale Publishers** and follow us on Twitter at **@Summersdale**.